# Reading Well 3

## John Cooper and George Livingstone

**Oliver & Boyd**

**Acknowledgments**
The author and publishers are grateful to the following for permission to reproduce extracts from the publications listed:

A & C Black Publishers: *People in History* by R. J. Unstead; Bell & Hyman Ltd: *Rivers* (*On Location Books*) by Margaret Slack; The Bodley Head Ltd: *The Knights of King Midas* by Paul Berna and *The Children of Totem Town* by Kaj Hemmelstrup; Jonathan Cape Ltd: *Emil and the Detective* by Erick Kästner (translated by Eileen Hall) and *Run for your Life* by David Line; William Collins Sons & Co. Ltd: *The Warden's Niece* by Gillian Avery and *The Moon of Gomrath* by Alan Garner; Faber & Faber Ltd: *The River at Green Knowe* by Lucy M. Boston and *The Turbulent Term of Tyke Tiler* by Gene Kemp; Victor Gollancz Ltd: *On the Run* by Nina Bawden; A. M. Heath & Co. Ltd: *The Kingdom under the Sea* by Joan Aiken (published by Jonathan Cape Ltd.); David Higham Associates Ltd: *The Dam Busters* by Paul Brickhill; Hodder & Stoughton Ltd: *The Latter Days* by P. R. Reid © 1953); Hutchinson & Co. (Publishers) Ltd: *Silver Brumby Whirlwind* by Flyne Mitchell; Michael Joseph Ltd: *Walkabout* by James Vance Marshall; Macdonald Educational Ltd: *United States of America* by John Bear and *Spain, the Land and its Peoples* (*Macdonald Countries* series); Macmillan, London and Basingstoke: *The Diddakoi* by Rumer Godden and *The Ogre Downstairs* and *Wilkin's Tooth* by Diana Wynne Jones; Transworld Publishers Ltd: *Air and Water* (*How and Why Books*) by M. L. Kean and C. Cunieff; Weidenfield and Nicolson Ltd/Arthur Barker: *Famous Arctic Adventures* by Len Ortzen.

*Illustrations by Nancy Bryce and Peter Chapel*

**Oliver & Boyd**
Robert Stevenson House
1–3 Baxter's Place
Leith Walk
Edinburgh EH1 3BB
*A Division of Longman Group Ltd*

First published 1983

© Oliver & Boyd 1983

All rights reserved. No part of this book may be reproduced, stored in a retrieval system or transmitted, in any form or by any means electronic, mechanical, photocopying, recording, or otherwise, without the prior permission of the Copyright Owner.

ISBN 0 05 003378 6

Printed in Hong Kong by
C & C Joint Printing Co., (H.K.) Ltd.

# Contents

|    | Preface | 4 |
|----|---------|---|
| 1  | Danger at Night | 5 |
| 2  | The Children of Totem Town | 7 |
| 3  | Alphabetical Order | 10 |
| 4  | Air | 12 |
| 5  | Main Ideas | 14 |
| 6  | Water | 16 |
| 7  | The Good Life | 18 |
| 8  | Using Rivers | 20 |
| 9  | Big Deal | 22 |
| 10 | Holiday Reports (Graphs) | 24 |
| 11 | Into the Water | 26 |
| 12 | Supporting Details | 28 |
| 13 | A Bouncing Bomb | 30 |
| 14 | The Dam Busters | 32 |
| 15 | Cause and Effect | 34 |
| 16 | On the Run | 36 |
| 17 | Fire! | 38 |
| 18 | Summarising | 40 |
| 19 | Escape from Colditz | 41 |
| 20 | River Rescue | 44 |
| 21 | Sequence and Instructions | 47 |
| 22 | Paper Hats | 48 |
| 23 | Into the Witch's Lair | 50 |
| 24 | Trailing a Thief | 52 |
| 25 | Arctic Explorers | 54 |
| 26 | The Moving Toffee-Bar | 56 |
| 27 | Context Clues | 58 |
| 28 | Unhappy Christmas | 60 |
| 29 | Eskimos Today | 62 |
| 30 | A Hard and Lonely Life | 64 |
| 31 | Inferences and Predicting Outcomes | 66 |
| 32 | Survivors | 68 |
| 33 | Tyke on the Roof | 70 |
| 34 | Fact and Opinion | 72 |
| 35 | Bull Fighting | 74 |
| 36 | Paradurra Megalocephala Abyssinienses | 76 |
| 37 | The Young David Livingstone | 78 |

# Preface

The materials in *Reading Well* are intended to assist pupils in the acquisition and development of higher order reading skills.

The authors have sought to include a wide range of writing for children of the relevant age group. Extracts from children's fiction are taken from a wide variety of writers. In making the selection regard was had to books which seemed to be popular in school and class libraries. Moreover, attempts have been made to select extracts which are interesting and might encourage pupils to read more of the books chosen. In all these extracts, quality was the major criterion for selection, but enjoyment played a strong part.

An almost equal amount of space has been given to non-fiction. Children require to consult such material as they read to learn. Such reading is particularly important in the field of environmental studies, and there is a deliberate attempt to focus on material which they may well use in this area of the curriculum.

The skills to be taught and/or developed are skimming, recognising the main idea in a paragraph, selecting details to support the main idea, summarising, following ideas or events in sequence, using context clues, distinguishing between fact and opinion, recognising cause and effect, and finding proof. For the convenience of teachers, the questions have been grouped under these headings.

Interspersed throughout the book are skills pages designed to help in the teaching of specific skills. Teachers may wish to use those pages in a sequence quite different from that found in the book, especially since each skill is used in units that appear before the teaching page and hence the teacher will wish to exercise discretion. It may be worth noting that each skill is practised in the unit that immediately follows that skill's teaching page.

It would be quite unrealistic to try deliberately to focus on every higher reading skill in every passage. Some of the questions in "Understanding the Passage" sections might well have appeared under other headings, but the intention is to ensure general understanding and to direct special attention to a few skills in each unit.

Many of the questions will lend themselves to much discussion and interaction because of differing interpretations by the pupils. Discussion will often be preceded by the questions in oral form. On other occasions the teacher may wish the pupils to write their answers in advance of discussion. In very many cases there will be alternative and competing answers.

As a rough guide, the sequence of units is in accordance with the increasing order of difficulty of reading content.

John Cooper and George Livingstone

# 1 Danger at Night

1. Colin never knew what woke him. He lay on his back and stared at the moonlight. He had woken suddenly and completely, with no buffer of drowsiness to take the shock. His senses were needle-pointed, ...

2. He got out of bed, and went to the window. Then he saw something move. He saw it only out of the corner of his eye, and it was gone in a moment, a shadow had slipped across the patch of moonlight.

3. Colin pulled on his shirt and trousers over his pyjamas, and jammed his feet into a pair of shoes, before going to wake Gowther. But when he came to Susan's door he paused, and, for no reason that he could explain, opened the door. The bed was empty, the window open.

4. Colin tiptoed downstairs and groped his way to the door. It was still bolted. Had Susan dropped nine feet to the cobbles? He eased the bolts, and stepped outside, and as he looked he saw a thin silhouette pass over the skyline of the Riddings.

5. Colin ran: and by the time he stood up at the top of Clinton hill he had halved the lead that Susan had gained. For it was undoubtedly Susan. She was wearing her pyjamas. Straight ahead of her were the dark tops of the trees in the quarry.

6. "Sue!" No, wait. That's dangerous. She's sleep-walking. But she's heading for the quarry. Colin ran as hard as he had ever run. He came to the fence that stood on the edge of the highest cliff and looked around while he recovered his breath.

7. The moon showed all the hill-side and much of the quarry: the pump-tower gleamed, and the vanes turned. But Susan was nowhere to be seen. Colin searched the sides of the quarry with his eyes, and looked at the smooth black mirror of the water. He was frightened. Where was she?

8. Then he cried out in fear as something slithered over his shoe and plucked at his ankle. He started back, and looked

down. It was a hand. A ledge of earth, inches wide, ran along the other side of the fence and crumbled away to the rock face a few feet below: then the drop was sheer to the tarn-like water. The hand now clutched the ledge.

"Sue!"

(From *The Moon of Gomrath* by Alan Garner)

## Questions

*Vocabulary*

Find words in the story which mean: (a) an outline of an object against the light *(paragraph 4)*, (b) blade of a propeller *(paragraph 7)*.

Check your answers in your dictionary.

*Understanding the story*

1. What do you think woke Colin?
2. Buffers are designed to take shocks. How would you feel if you were affected by a "buffer of drowsiness"? How would you react to sounds?
3. What explanation would you give for Colin putting on his clothes on top of his pyjamas?
4. Why do you think Colin did not shout to Sue from the window?
5. What suggests that Sue was sleep-walking?
6. For what purpose might the vanes and pump-tower be used?
7. What great danger did Colin escape?

*Figures of speech*

1. How are Colin's senses described? What does this mean?
2. To what is the water in the quarry compared in paragraph 7? Are the words "like" or "as" used?
3. How is the water described in paragraph 8?

*Details* (See pages 28 to 29.)

From the story, is each of the following statements *True, False or* doesn't the story say?
1. It was a moonlit night.
2. Susan had dropped nine feet from her window.
3. Sue often sleep-walked.
4. There were no trees in the quarry.
5. The side of the quarry was very steep.

# 2 The Children of Totem Town

A. (This appeared on the cover of the book to encourage people to read it.)

An enormous bulldozer was crawling towards the field. It came from the building site and advanced slowly but steadily. Smoke rose from its funnel in long black puffs, and the large sharp-toothed shovel was held menacingly high. It looked like a giant insect in search of prey.

At the edge of the hut village it turned on its caterpillar feet with a crunching noise, and pushed its nose against the palisades.

Slowly it lowered the blade and began moving forward.

Was this really going to be the end of the village—or would their plans to save it work?

B. (This is part of the story in the book.)

But there was no staff.

The town engineer's expression changed. "It should be right there," he shouted.

"Yes," said the man, "but it isn't."

"But where is it?" cried the town engineer.

"I don't know," said the driver, trying hard not to smile. "That's exactly what I couldn't understand."

The town engineer looked angrily at him.

"There must be a mistake," he said, trying to keep calm. He glanced again at the plan and walked a bit further. It didn't take him long to realise that the staffs were in total confusion.

"Well, where do you want me to drive then, guv?" asked

the man with a hint of sarcasm in his voice. "You said I must be stupid not to ..."

"That's enough," hissed the town engineer. He strode in among the staffs but was soon back. His lips were tightly pressed together and his eyes looked steely.

"It was done on purpose," he said hoarsely. "Sheer hooliganism!"

"I wouldn't be so sure of that," said the man. "It might be the work of a drunk."

"It's those damned kids," snorted the town engineer. "But they'll get their come-uppance," he added menacingly. "For the time being you can do the edges, and I'll see to it that the ground is properly staked out again."

He got into his car and shot off. . . .

(From *The Children of Totem Town* by Kaj Hemmelstrup)

### Questions

*Context clues* (See pages 58 to 59.)

Look for clues in the passages to help you decide which is the correct meaning for each word.

| | Words | | Meanings |
|---|---|---|---|
| 1. | menacingly | (a) | fence of stakes driven into the ground |
| 2. | palisades | (b) | what they deserve |
| 3. | sarcasm | (c) | criminal work done by street roughs |
| 4. | hooliganism | (d) | in a manner threatening great danger |
| 5. | come-uppance | (e) | hurtful remark said in scorn |

*Understanding the story*

(Extract A is a part of an advertisement encouraging readers to read the book. Extract B is part of the story.)
1. Why do you think the hut village was to be destroyed?
2. Why would the palisades have been built?
3. How would the driver and engineer know the staffs were in the wrong places?
4. Which words tell us that the staffs were seriously out of position?
5. Apart from what he said, how could you have told that the engineer was very angry?
6. What did the engineer seem to be suggesting would happen to the children?

*Reading for detail*

*From the story, decide whether each of the following statements is* true (T), false (F), *or* whether the story doesn't say (DS)?
1. The bulldozer came from the building site.
2. The palisades were damaged.
3. The staffs had been disarranged.
4. The driver needed the stakes to guide him.
5. The town engineer found the whole episode amusing.

*Sarcasm*

*Sarcasm is a bitter remark, meaning the opposite of what is said and intended to hurt one's feelings.*
   eg The driver appeared to be agreeing he was stupid but what was he really suggesting?

*Which of the following statements would have been sarcastic?*

*Driver to engineer*
1. "You made a great job of putting up the stakes."
2. "I can't see where I am supposed to drive the bulldozer."
3. "That must be a good plan you drew."

*Engineer to driver*
4. "A blind man could see where to drive the bulldozer."
5. "You cannot complete the job until the stakes are put in their proper places."
6. "You should use your intelligence if you have any."

*Predicting outcomes* (See page 66.)

1. What do you think the engineer did when he shot off?
2. The children had plans. Which other plans might they have had?
3. What do you think happened to the village in the end?

# 3 Alphabetical Order

A B C D E F G H I J K L M N O P Q R S T U V W X Y Z

In indexes and pages of dictionaries and encyclopedias we find words are written in alphabetical order. This has been done to make it easy for us to find the word we may be looking for, but it will be easy only if we can put words in alphabetical order.

A. 1. James is going to find out more about (a) stars, (b) clouds, (c) moon, (d) planets.
   *In which order will he find them in an encyclopedia?*

2. Mary is taking part in a project on water. She wishes to find out more about (a) seas, (b) rivers, (c) lakes, (d) oceans.
   *In which order will they appear in an encyclopedia?*

3. It is more difficult when all the words begin with the same letter. If James had been looking up (a) guard, (b) gate, (c) general, (d) grenadier, he would have noted that they all begin with *g* and he would arrange them in order according to the second letters.
   *What would be that order?*

4. Mary might find it more difficult still if she had to look up (a) copper, (b) aluminium, (c) gold, (d) silver, (e) platinum, (f) steel, (g) chrome. (Some words begin with the same letter, other words with different letters.)
   *What would be the correct alphabetical order?*

5. *In which order would the following words appear in a dictionary?*
   girl, birthday, children, party, enjoyment, cakes, baking, games, fun.

B. 1. It was in a church in Dumfries that Bruce and Comyn met. Bruce accused Comyn of betraying him to the English King. Comyn, terrified of Bruce's anger, denied it, but the proof was too strong. Drawing his dagger, Bruce stabbed Comyn to death. As Balliol had fled to France seven years before, Bruce was now the only important claimant to the throne of Scotland.

*Arrange in alphabetical order:*
(a) Dumfries  Bruce  Comyn  English  Balliol  Scotland
(b) church  betrayal  terror  anger  proof  dagger  death  claimant  throne

2. *The Final Ascent*
Actually the final ascent on the mountain was due to be attempted during the following day. After hearing that the forecast suggested mild conditions and knowing that all necessary preparations had been made, George decided that the party would turn in before 10 o'clock and set out at four in the morning.

*Find the word in the above paragraph which means:*
last,  climbing up,  tried,  next,  not cold,  things made ready,  made up his mind

*Write out in alphabetical order the seven words you found in the paragraph above and also write out the meaning of each word beside it.*

3. David awoke very early but disturbed no one because it was important for everyone to get as much rest as possible. Light snow was falling and the wind had almost died down but it was bitterly cold. There was no sound except the flapping of the tent and men breathing as they slept.

*Find the word in the above paragraph which means:*
stopped sleeping,  awakened,  necessary,  extremely,  apart from,  sound made by moving.

*Rewrite the six words you found in the paragraph in alphabetical order, and write out the meaning of each word beside it.*

# 4 Air

1. It may seem hard to believe that air takes up space, but you can easily show that this is true. All you need is an ordinary drinking glass and a pail of water. The glass looks empty. If you were to show the glass to a friend and ask him what is in the glass, he would probably say, "Nothing," or, "It's empty." Put your hand in the glass. There seems to be nothing there; the glass certainly *feels* empty.

2. Now turn the glass upside down and push it down into the pail of water. Be sure you hold the glass perfectly straight. Do not tilt it to one side. Push the glass down into the water until all of it is under water. Now look closely. You will see that only a small amount of water has risen into the glass. The rest of the glass is filled with air. The air is taking up the space inside the glass, and the water cannot fill it.

3. The experiment you just performed with the glass and the pail of water showed you that water could not get into the glass as long as there was air inside it. This fact is used by men who must work under water. Perhaps the men must dig holes for the foundation of a bridge or a dam, or perhaps they must repair a sunken ship. They can do this and still remain dry by working inside a diving bell. A diving bell looks like a large iron bell. It is lowered beneath the water—open end down—until it rests on the bottom. Because the diving bell is filled with air, water does not rise into it, just as water did not rise into the glass. Air is taking up space inside the diving bell and water cannot take up the same space.

(From *Air and Water* (*The How and Why Books*) by M. L. Keen and C. Cunniff)

## Questions

Context clues (See page 58.)

*Find the word in the passage which means:* (a) normal, common, (b) test to find if something works *(paragraph 3)*, (c) base on which something rests *(paragraph 3)*.

*Details* (See page 28.)

*According to the passage, is each of the following statements* True *or* False *or is it the case that the passage* Doesn't Say?
1. There *seems* to be nothing in an empty glass.
2. An empty glass has nothing in it.
3. A glass that feels empty is full of air.
4. Only a small amount of water will rise into an upturned glass which is pushed deep into a pail of water.
5. (a) If you slightly tilt the upturned glass which you hold in a pail of water, some air will escape.
   (b) As you continue to tilt the glass, more air will escape.
   (c) When all the air has escaped, the glass will be full of water.
6. (a) Men sometimes use diving bells when working on wrecks.
   (b) Men sometimes use diving bells when studying living things in the sea.

*Following directions* (See page 47.)

*Complete each instruction as you would give it to a person trying the experiment to see if air takes up space. Write the whole sentence out in your own book.*
1. You require . . . .
2. Fill the pail with . . . .
3. Make sure . . . is empty.
4. Turn the glass . . . .
5. Push the glass into the . . . making sure you keep it . . . .

*Find out for yourself*

1. Try the experiment. Try to find out whether Details 5(a), 5(b), and 5(c) are true or false. (The passage did not say, so you don't need to change the answers you gave earlier.)
2. Find out how air is kept fresh in a diving bell when men are working inside.
3. Some water will rise into a diving bell (as it did in the glass). If men are to work in a diving bell and remain dry, no water at all should enter. How is it kept free of water?

*Alphabetical order* (See page 10.)

*Arrange the following words in alphabetical order:*
    air   water   glass   pail   space   empty   diver   bell

# 5 Main Ideas

1. *Below are three groups of pictures. What do the pictures in each group have in common? (The first one is done for you.)*

    (a)  (They are all *Motor Cars*)

    (b)

    (c)

2. *What do the words in each group have in common? (The first one is done for you.)*
    - (a) elm, beech, ash, sycamore *(Trees)*
    - (b) coal, wood, coke, peat
    - (c) rugs, mats, carpets, linoleum
    - (d) beef, mutton, pork, venison
    - (e) tin, iron, gold, silver
    - (f) leeks, carrots, turnips

3. *When Anne drew the sketches below was she thinking mainly about:*
    (a) giraffes, or  (b) elephants, or  (c) animals of Africa?

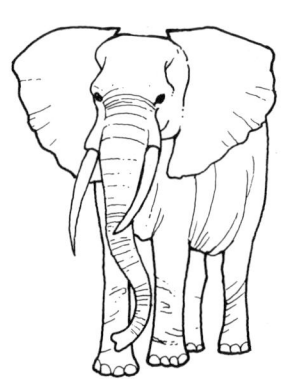

4. *When a writer writes a paragraph there is usually a main thought in his mind. Read each paragraph carefully and decide which of the choices below would be correct.*

   A. Stone Age people had a struggle to find enough food. They lived on fruits, berries, shellfish and the meat of any animals they were able to kill.

   *This paragraph is mainly about:* (a) berries, (b) Stone Age people's food, (c) shellfish.

   B. In those days there lived in Britain lions, hippopotami, elephants and many other wild animals which have disappeared from the scene long ago.

   *This paragraph is mainly about:* (a) elephants, (b) wild animals of long ago, (c) this country.

   C. The home of the Stone Age family who lived in this wild country was a cave or perhaps a shelter among the rocks. It was a very poor type of dwelling, even if the climate was warmer at that time.

   *This paragraph is mainly about:* (a) the wild country, (b) the climate, (c) the home of the Stone Age family.

5. Last Thursday's fog caused many delays. There were long queues of traffic on the outskirts of the town as commuters drove in slowly. For three hours all aircraft were grounded except for a few helicopters. Even main line trains were running late.

   *Is the above paragraph mainly about:* (a) fog, (b) how people travel to work, (c) effects of fog upon travellers?

6. Mary soon learned that mountaineering demanded physical fitness. In the first place there were many hours of just walking with very few rest periods. Secondly some parts were so steep that it was very tiring to climb, even with the aid of ropes. Thirdly she found that carrying equipment was very much an added burden.

   *What is the above paragraph mainly about?*

# 6 Water

*Skimming*

Here are six paragraphs about water. They deal with: (a) water in your <u>daily life</u>, (b) water as a source of <u>power</u>, (c) <u>weather</u> affected by water, (d) water in your <u>body</u>, (e) <u>food</u> depending on water, (f) water shaping the <u>surface of the earth</u>.
*Write out a column (a) to (f) and write down the key words which have been underlined against each letter.*

Take them one at a time and skim through the passage to find which paragraph deals with each one. Write out the paragraph number for each when you spot it.

1. All living things contain water. More than two thirds of your body is made up of water. The water in your body helps dissolve the food you eat, which is then carried in the blood to your living cells. Water also helps carry away the dissolved waste materials from the cells. And water helps to keep your body at the right temperature.
2. Water is important not only inside your body, but in your daily life as well. It is used for cooking, bathing, washing clothes and dishes, and cleaning. And water provides recreation such as swimming, sailing, or water-skiing.
3. Plants, too, must have water. No plant can grow without water. This means that all our food depends on water because all food—even meat, which is the flesh of plant-eating animals—comes from plants.
4. Water is an important source of power. Man uses the force of running water to turn the wheels of mills and to make electricity.
5. Water shapes the surface of the earth. Time and again, the force of the running waters of streams and rivers has worn down whole mountain ranges until they became flat plains. And the pounding of ocean waves on the shores has shaped the coastlines of all the continents.
6. Much of our weather is due to the amount of water in the air. Clouds, fog, dew, rain, snow, and sleet are forms of water in the air. Moving air causes most of the changes in weather. As wind blows warm or cold, damp or dry, the weather changes.

(From *Air and Water* (*The How and Why Wonder Books*)
by M. L. Keen and C. Cunniff)

*Main ideas and supporting details* (See page 28.)

*Complete by writing down the details in your own book.*
1. *Paragraph 1 is mainly about* the importance of water in your body.
   Details (a) ... (b) ... (c) ...
2. *Paragraph 2 is mainly about* the importance of water in daily life.
   Details (a) ... (b) ... (c) ... (d) ... (e) ...

*Cause and effect* (See page 34.)

*Complete in your own words by writing the whole sentence in your own book.*
1. Some mountains become flat plains because ....
2. The present shape of the coast lines has been caused partly by ....
3. Plants must have water because ....

*Sequence* (See page 47.)

*Fill in the blanks in each sentence. Write the whole sentence in your own book.*
1. Water falls as ....
2. Some animals eat the ....
3. ... makes plants grow.
4. We eat the ... of animals.

Re-arrange the above four sentences in the order in which they would happen.

*Alphabetical order*

The last paragraph mentions six forms of water in weather.
*Write them out in the order in which they might appear in an index.*

# 7 The Good Life

1. Once there was a poor young nobleman who had nothing in the world but a ruined castle in the forest, a horse, and a hound. So he was obliged to go hunting every day, in order to get his food. However, he looked after his animals with great care, brushing and combing them every evening, giving them the same food as he had himself, and chopping wood to make a fire so that they should be warm at night. In consequence of this they loved him dearly.
2. One day the young lord went hunting with his hound in a densely thicketed part of the forest. He tied his horse to a tree outside this bushy patch and left him grazing.
3. Presently a fox came by and stopped to admire the horse.
4. "My word, brother, you seem fat and glossy! Your master must look after you well."
5. "Indeed he does," said the horse. "Everything he has, I share."
6. "May I sit here for a while and keep you company?" asked the fox.
7. "By all means," replied the horse politely. So the fox sat down by him and chatted until the young lord came back with a stag which he had shot. He was rather astonished to see the fox, and raised his gun, at which the fox exclaimed,
8. "Don't shoot, my dear sir! Rather, take me into your service, and I'll keep an eye on your horse for you while you are off hunting. Good gracious! What a risky thing to leave a horse tied up here, when there are so many wolves and bears in the forest!"
9. The young lord thought this was sensible advice; he allowed the fox to come home with him, running alongside his hound. And when they arrived back at the ruined castle the fox was given a share of the supper and a place by the fire. "I certainly am in luck!" she thought.

(From *The Kingdom under the Sea* by Joan Aiken)

**Questions**

*Understanding the story*

1. For what would the nobleman use: (a) the horse, and (b) the hound, when he was hunting?
2. Brushing and combing the animals each day is a sign of good care. Why do you think this should be done?
3. He shared his food with the animals. Suggest two things in our diet which would not be eaten by horses.
4. What is the horse eating in the story?
5. Why would you be unable to believe this story?
6. The nobleman returned with a stag. Which of the following would be likely to enjoy the meat of the stag: (a) the nobleman, (b) the hound, (c) the horse, (d) the fox?
7. If this story were true, why would it not be happening in this country today?
8. In what way was the advice of the fox sensible?
9. The nobleman was said to possess only a castle, a horse and a hound. What else must he have had if the story is to be believed?

*Cause and effect* (See page 34.)

*Complete the following by writing the whole sentence in your own book. Read the story again for clues.*
1. . . . because he had only a ruined castle, a horse and a hound.
2. . . . because he looked after them very well.
3. . . . because the horse looked fat and glossy.
4. . . . because it had given good advice.
5. . . . because it was given supper and a place by the fire.

*Main ideas*

1. Does paragraph 1 deal mainly with
     (a) the ruined castle,
     (b) why the animals liked the nobleman,
   or (c) chopping wood for the fire?
2. Does paragraph 8 deal mainly with
     (a) the fox being a great help to the lord,
   or (b) bears in the forest?
3. Paragraph 9 deals mainly with "the fox's experiences after convincing the lord".
   What are the details? (a) . . . , (b) . . . , (c) . . . .
   Write them down in your own book.

# 8 Using Rivers

1. From the earliest days of history people have made use of rivers. No doubt men caught fish in them in the Old Stone Age. Later on, when men had learnt how to make boats they fished from these. When they had caught all the fish they could in one part of the river they would move to another, carrying their light-weight boats on their backs.
2. The Angles and Saxons who came from North Germany in the fifth, sixth and seventh centuries, that is from about AD 400–700, used the rivers that flow into the North Sea to sail as far inland as possible. Later, in the ninth century, the Vikings who came from Denmark and Norway used these rivers for the same purpose. At first these invaders came to raid and to explore. Later they came to stay.
3. Having decided to settle, they would look round for somewhere suitable to build houses. They would need a place fairly near water but not near enough to be flooded if there was heavy rain. They would choose ground that was high enough to be dry but not so high that it was cold and windy. They needed, too, a place in which the soil was light enough to plough and grow crops. No doubt many such places would be in river valleys and it was here that they built their houses and villages. When they visited neighbours further along the valley they would find the easiest way. They would then tell

their fellow villagers who later used the same route and so on. In time a footpath was made along the riverside.

4. Have you seen any castles near rivers? Castles often *were* built near rivers. One way in which they could get rid of their sewage was to let it flow straight into the river. So you see even in the Middle Ages there was pollution. Why wasn't pollution then such a problem as it is now? If you think hard you can find at least two reasons. But getting rid of sewage was not the most important reason for putting castles near water. What was it?

(From *Rivers* (*On Location Books*)
by Margaret Slack)


## Questions

*Understanding the passage*

*Which word or phrase has been missed out in each of the following sentences?*
1. To survive people must have . . . . Stone Age people got some of theirs from the rivers.
2. When the first Vikings sailed up the rivers they came in order to . . . .
3. As well as food people need . . . in order to survive. This is one reason why Vikings settled in river valleys.

*Details*

*Is each of the following statements* True, False, *or is it the case that the passage* Doesn't Say?
1. Stone Age men made boats of leather stretched round a wicker framework.
2. Vikings knew how to cultivate land and grow crops.
3. The Vikings came before the Angles and Saxons.

*The reason why*

1. Why was pollution not so much of a problem at the time of the Vikings? What are two reasons?
2. What do you think is the main reason why castles were built beside rivers?
3. How do you think footpaths were made along the rivers?
4. Paragraph 3 gives reasons why Vikings settled in river valleys. What are three of those reasons?

# 9 Big Deal

"We've got some fish, jolly good it is too," Frisquet began. "Do you want any?"

"Let's see it," said the chef suspiciously.

They unstrapped the two baskets and emptied their contents fish by fish on to the kitchen table. There was still some life in one of the bass and he gave one last flip of his tail to warrant the freshness of the catch. The chef whistled under his breath.

"There's enough there for thirty helpings at least," he said in a low voice. "Each of the bass will do a table for six." ...

"How much do you want?" asked the chef, turning to the children.

"Five thousand francs," Rouqui answered. ...

The chef gave a piercing cry as though cut to the quick by the price.

"It's too dear! I'd never show a profit on that! I'll give you two thousand, and that's over-paying you."

Rouqui was so shy that he would have yielded had Frisquet given him the chance.

"One of our friends' fathers caught them," said the latter, "and he fixed the price, not us. If it's too much for you we'll go on to Bandol!"

Rouqui held out his hand and took the big bank note. It was clearly new. Five thousand francs! For the moment he stood still, staring blankly in front of him.

"You've got the golden touch," Frisquet whispered as they pushed the bicycle out of the yard. "We should have put our price up." ...

Rigolo's rickety old bicycle bounced crazily across the ruts of the Pointe Espagnole, roared down the last slope, swept up the headland to the gun emplacement, and collapsed at the door, depositing its riders in the bushes.

"Well?" asked Rigolo, who was standing guard outside.

He let them pass. The whole gang was there pressed tightly into the dank smelling den, talking shrill-voiced like a litter of fox-cubs. Wordlessly Rouqui unfolded the bank note and it was passed from hand to hand in awestruck silence.

(From *The Knights of King Midas* by Paul Berna)

**Questions**

*Vocabulary*

*Find words in the story which mean:* (a) imagining something wrong, (b) guarantee, (c) sharp, (d) given in, (e) platform for a gun.

*Check the words in your dictionary.*

*Understanding the story*

1. What might make the chef speak suspiciously when the boys asked if he wanted fish?
2. What suggests the fish had been caught recently?
3. How many bass would they have had?
4. What message would the chef's piercing cry be intended to convey to the boys?
5. Do you believe that the chef would not make a profit if he paid 5000 francs? Why?
6. What effect did the threat to go to Bandol have?
7. What did Frisquet mean when he said Rouqui had the golden touch?
8. Why would there be such a silence as the note was passed round?

*Making inferences* (See page 66.)

*What inferences might you draw from each of the following?*
1. Frisquet gave Rouqui no chance to agree to 2000 francs.
2. Frisquet said a friend's father caught the fish and fixed the price.
3. Rouqui stood still, staring in front of him when he received the money.
4. The boys departed in a great hurry.
5. Rigolo was standing on guard.
6. The gang met in a dank smelling den.

# 10 Holiday Reports (Graphs)

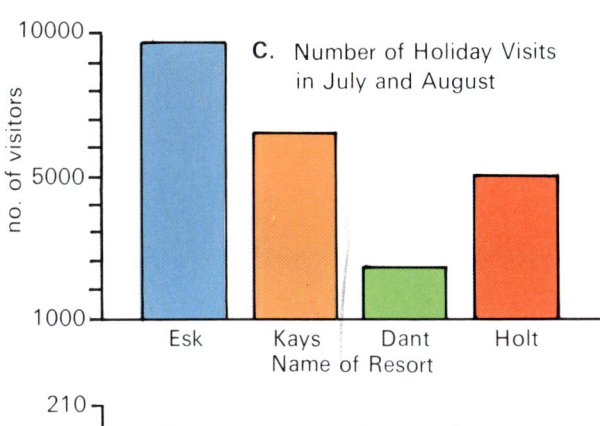

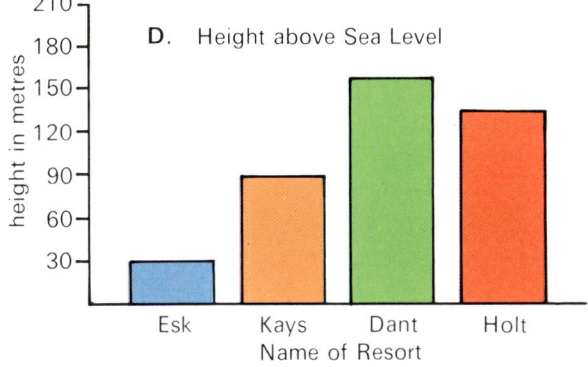

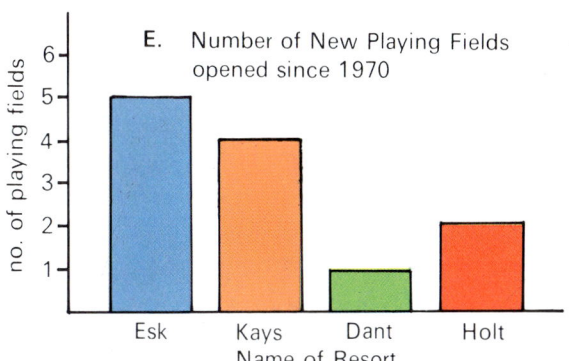

## Questions

*Put them in order*

*Write the answers in your own book.*
1. Arrange the four resorts in order of hours of sunshine, starting with the one with fewest hours.
2. Arrange the resorts in hours of rainfall, starting with the one with the smallest rainfall.
3. Arrange the resorts in order of numbers of summer visitors, starting with the village which attracts the fewest.
4. Arrange the resorts in order of height above sea level, starting with the resort that is nearest to sea level.

*Inferences* (See page 66.)

(a) Write a sentence to say what you notice when you compare your answers to numbers 1 and 2 above?
(b) What do you notice about your answers to numbers 1 and 3? What inference do you draw?
(c) Compare your answers to numbers 2 and 4 above. What inference do you draw?
(d) Compare graphs A, C and E. What inference do you draw?

# 11 Into the Water

1. Thowra heard Yuri's neigh of horror just before he saw a tear-misted vision of water below them.
2. She was going too fast on such a steep slope: the wind came stronger than ever: it caught Yuri, it caught Thowra. Their hooves were barely touching the steep rocks, then they were no longer touching. They were no longer galloping on rocks and earth, they were out in the wild stream of air—and dropping fast towards the turbulent water of the lake.
3. Thowra saw Yuri hit the water and submerge, just before he hit it himself. He went in with such force that he was under the surface in an instant and going down—water filling ears and nose, weight of water pressing against his body. Instinctively he started the motions of swimming. His legs could barely move against the pressure of water, but he could feel himself stop sinking and start upwards again.
4. He swam desperately, as though climbing up the water. Then suddenly his head broke the surface. Air! He took a huge gulp ... and kept on swimming.
5. Yuri was not there. His heart lurched with fear, but then her head came up, gasping. A wave broke over her. When her nose got above the froth and foam, her nostrils were dilated with terror and her gasps were even more desperate.
6. "Yuri! Yuri!" Thowra called her.
7. The smooth lake was unrecognizable. The wind was whipping it to higher and higher waves that slapped at the side of his head.... Slap of cold water, slap. Sometimes waves were right over his ears.

(From *Silver Brumby Whirlwind* by Flyne Mitchell)

**Questions**

*Context clues* (See page 58.)

*The following words are used in the story. Look for clues to help you to decide which is the correct meaning of each word.*

| | Words | | | | Meanings |
|---|---|---|---|---|---|
| 1. | vision | *(paragraph 1)* | (a) | sink | |
| 2. | turbulent | *(paragraph 2)* | (b) | naturally without thinking | |
| 3. | submerge | *(paragraph 3)* | (c) | sight | |
| 4. | dilated | *(paragraph 5)* | (d) | restless and noisy | |
| 5. | instinctively | *(paragraph 3)* | (e) | swollen, wide | |

*Understanding the story*

1. Which one do you think saw the lake first? Which words suggest the answer?
2. What was Yuri? Which is the first word to give you the clue?
3. What happened as a result of the steepness of the rocks?
4. Why would Thowra go down so far so quickly?
5. Which word tells us that his ability to swim was not the result of much practice?
6. Which words describe Thowra's state of fear (paragraph 5)?
7. Which words suggest that Yuri was even more terrified?
8. What, as much as poor swimming ability, might cause both to drown?

*Cause and effect* (See page 34.)

*Complete each of the following (write out the whole sentence each time):*
1. They were flying through the air because they had . . . .
2. At first Thowra could hardly move his legs in the water because . . . .
3. Yuri was very afraid because . . . .
4. The smooth lake was unrecognisable because . . . .

*Alphabetical order*

*Arrange the following words in their alphabetical order. (Write out each word once only.)*

horses   gallop   hooves   swim   waves   water   lake   pressure

# 12 Supporting Details

When we have recognised the main idea it is more easy to remember the supporting details.

1. *Write out three details for each of the following. (The first one is done for you.)*

   (a) Footwear  *Details* (a) boots  (b) slippers  (c) shoes

   (b) Furniture  *Details* (a) . . .  (b) . . .  (c) . . .

   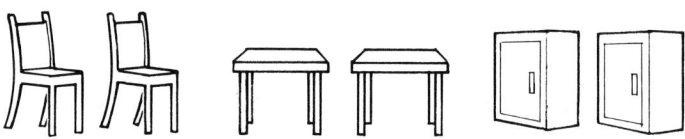

   (c) Dishes  *Details* (a) . . .  (b) . . .  (c) . . .

   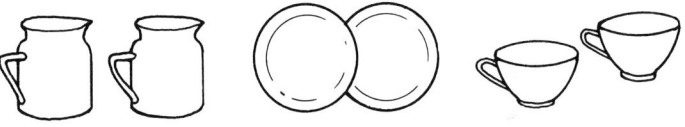

2. *Read the following paragraph. You are given the main idea and one supporting detail. Copy them down and add another two supporting details.*

   To be strong and healthy you need to take plenty of exercise. Walking is one of the best forms of exercise and much better for you than sitting in a car. There are plenty of games such as football and tennis which will keep you fit. Perhaps you would enjoy hill climbing as it will strengthen your muscles and ensure you get fresh air.

   *This paragraph is mainly about:* Forms of exercise which could give you fitness.
   *Details* (a) Walking, (b) . . . , (c) . . .

3. *Read the following paragraph. You are given the main idea, copy it down and add four supporting details.*

One can easily call to mind some of the many sports staged at Wembley Stadium. Amateur and professional boxers from all over the world have fought there. Not only do we see British National swimming championships but many international swimmers as well. The whole range of athletics is catered for too. People from many countries came to see or participate in the Olympic Games in 1948 which were staged at Wembley.

*The above paragraph is mainly about:* Some of the sporting events staged at Wembley.
*Details:* (a) . . . , (b) . . . , (c) . . .

4. *Read the following paragraph and state the main idea (you are given the supporting details).*

James put forward the arguments why his father should allow him to go to camp. He had already saved the money which was one of the main considerations. Mr Philips, the headmaster, had agreed that leave of absence could be granted. Peter and David, his two best friends, had already been given permission to go. Anyhow this would be the last opportunity James would have of going. His father sat listening but said nothing.

*This paragraph is mainly about:* . . . ?
*Details:* (a) he had saved the money
(b) he could get leave of absence
(c) his best friends were going
(d) this was his last chance

# 13 A Bouncing Bomb

1. "A bouncing bomb! A bomb which bounces on water! The man must be mad!"
2. Lots of British experts said this about an inventor called Barnes Wallis during 1942. For Wallis wanted to make a very unusual bomb. It was wartime and night after night, day after day, planes were leaving the shores of Britain to bomb targets in Germany. They attacked military camps, railway yards and weapon factories. They flew high up, dropping cigar-shaped bombs with large fins at one end. Such bombs fell with an awful, screaming sound. How could they bounce on water?
3. But the "bouncing bomb" man had an answer to this question.
4. "My bomb will not be the usual shape. It will be shaped like a large dustbin and it will bounce because it will be made to spin backwards before it leaves the plane. It will bounce just as a stone skids across water," he replied.
5. It seemed a crazy idea yet all the British experts knew that something different was needed. In a part of Germany known as the Ruhr were three huge dams, the Moehne, the Eder and the Sohne. If they could be smashed millions of tons of water would flood into the Ruhr, damaging factories and railway yards. All three were far too strong to be broken by ordinary bombs. The Moehne dam was made of concrete and was over one hundred metres thick at its base. The Eder and Sohne dams were just as strong.
6. The Germans knew that ordinary bombs could not break their dams. They thought that planes might try to drop torpedoes so they had large wire nets placed in the water in front of each dam. This is why Barnes Wallis had thought of a bouncing bomb. Such a bomb would bounce over the water and over the nets. Then, according to Wallis, the bomb would roll down the side of the dam and explode underwater. This

would set up shock waves so great that even the walls of the German dams would be broken.

7. A bouncing bomb, a bomb with a backward spin! A bomb that would crawl down the side of a dam. It seemed a crazy idea. Could it ever work?

(From Wide Range History Book 4<br>by L. E. Snellgrove)

## Questions

*Understanding the passage*

1. In what ways would ordinary bombs have helped to defeat the Germans?
2. In what ways would a burst dam have much the same effect as exploding bombs?
3. Why would (a) ordinary bombs and (b) torpedoes be unsuitable for attacking the dam?

*Supporting details*

*Your are given the main ideas for paragraphs 2, 4 and 5. Write out the supporting details for each. (Questions are asked to help you to find the answers.)*

*Paragraph 2 is about* the bombing of targets in Germany.
Details  (a)  Why did the planes set out?
         (b)  What did they attack?
         (c)  How would you describe the bombs?

*Paragraph 4 is about* how the proposed new bomb could be made to bounce.
Details  (a)  What would be its shape?
         (b)  What would it do before leaving the plane?
         (c)  What would happen when it hit the water?

*Paragraph 5 is mainly about* why it was desirable and difficult to attack the dams.
Details  (a)  Which dams were there and where?
         (b)  Why destroy the dams?
         (c)  Why were they difficult to destroy?

*Predicting outcomes* (See page 66.)

What do you think happened next? Do you think he built the bouncing bomb? Would it be a success? *Check up from books in the library.*

# 14 The Dam Busters

1. In the morning 617 Squadron went on leave, three days for the ground crew, seven days for the aircrew survivors—except Gibson, who stayed on two days to write to the mothers of the dead. He wrote to all 56 of them in his own hand.
2. In London and in their homes the crews found they were famous, though the headlines in Germany did not praise them. A plane had arrived back from over Germany with the first pictures of the damage, and they were breathtaking. The Moehne and Eder lakes were empty and 330 million tons of water were spreading like a cancer through the western Ruhr valleys. The bones of towns and villages lay lifeless. ...
3. A hundred and twenty-five factories were either destroyed or badly damaged, nearly 3000 hectares of farming land were ruined, twenty-five bridges had vanished, and twenty-one more were badly damaged. 6500 cattle and pigs were lost. But sadly 1294 people were drowned in the floods, and most were civilians. Most were not Germans—there were 749 slaves and prisoners among the dead. ...
4. After the raid the Germans moved hundreds of soldiers with flak guns to guard all the other dams in Germany. While they were working like beavers to repair the Moehne they also built two tall pylons 2000 yards back from the dam wall and strung between them a heavy cable across the lake. From this other cables dangled to the water, and lashed to them were contact grenades to catch low-flying aircraft. They strung two heavy anti-torpedo nets near the dam wall, and another one 1000 yards away.
5. But it was too late. The stable door was shut, but the horse had gone.

(Adapted from *The Dam Busters* by Paul Brickhill)

## Questions

*Main ideas and supporting details*

*Copy down the main idea for each paragraph below and add the details.*

*Paragraph 3 is mainly about:*
The damage that was caused.
Details   1. . . . ,   2. . . . ,   3. . . . ,   4. . . . ,   5. . . .

*Paragraph 4 is mainly about:*
How they improved the defences of the Moehne dam.
Details   1. . . . ,   2. . . . ,   3. . . .

*Cause and effect* (See page 34.)

*What do you think would be the reasons for each of the following?*
1. The aircrew survivors were given seven days leave but the ground staff only three days.
2. Barnes Wallis, the inventor of the bombs used, might have felt pleased.
3. Barnes Wallis might have felt very sad.

*Inferences* (See page 66.)

1. Paragraph 1 suggests that it was thought that 56 airmen died. A later account says only 53 died. What do you think is the reason for the difference?
2. Who might have commanded 617 squadron? Why do you think so?
3. What might lead us to think that the planes attacked at low level?

*Figures of speech*

1. The pictures were "breathtaking". Probably they did not really take anyone's breath away. What does this expression mean?
2. What do you think is meant by "the bones of towns and villages"?
3. What is meant by "working like beavers"? Why might this be a good description in this case?
4. Study the last sentence.
   They were not really shutting the stable door. They were building defences for the dam.
   What does it mean to say "but the horse had gone"?

# 15 Cause and Effect

Often when a writer is stating his ideas, he also gives the reasons or causes. Usually there are joining words such as *because, since* and *as* with which he begins to give the reason or cause.

*Consider the following sentence:*

Jane was happy because she was to go on a trip abroad.
Why was she happy? "because she was to go on a trip abroad".

1. *Complete each sentence (a) to (d). Think of a suitable cause or reason. Write out the whole sentence each time.*
   (a) James was suffering from sunstroke because . . . .
   (b) Wilma had no money left as . . . .
   (c) Charles did well in school because . . . .
   (d) June did not pass the piano examination because . . . .

2. *After reading the three short paragraphs below, answer the questions underneath them.*

   Jack intended staying where he was but he became so worried that he at last decided to walk down to the town. Outside Mr Peter's shop he stopped and waited as he knew Will would be inside the house next door.
   
   He hoped Will would stay there as there was no one else to attend to the phone if it rang. Mr Davies would be highly suspicious if no one answered the phone.
   
   Jack could not risk going inside as he was afraid he might have been followed. He would stay where he was as he could give the alarm if anyone approached.

*Answer each of the following five questions. (Do not begin your answer with the word "because".)*
(a) Why did Jack decide to walk down to the town?
(b) Why did Jack stop outside Mr Peter's shop?
(c) Why did Jack hope Will would stay inside the house?
(d) What might be the cause of Mr Davies becoming suspicious?
(e) Why did Jack decide to stay outside Mr Peter's shop?

3. *After reading the paragraph below write what was the cause of:*
(a) there being no unemployment, (b) there being so many tourists, (c) July being so popular for tourists, (d) tennis players coming in August.

There was no unemployment because there was so much work in the hotels at that time of year. Tourists came in their thousands as the weather was usually good. The most popular time was mid-July because the local gala was held at that time. Tennis players tended to come in August since that was the month of the tennis tournament.

# 16 On the Run

1. Ben moved cautiously towards the house. All the windows were dark; black squares in the blackness of the house wall. Ben stood at the foot of the fire-escape, looking up. Perhaps he could find Thomas's bedroom. Thomas was almost certain to be in bed by now. Miss Fisher wasn't the sort of woman to let a boy stay up late. If he could find Thomas's bedroom he could tell him the good news and go straight home, quick and silent as a thief in the night. . . .

2. But as he climbed the first flight of rusty, iron stairs, Ben's heart was pounding. Suppose Miss Fisher were to catch him—or one of the Uncles. The terrible Uncle Tuku in his Chief's robes! Ben thought about Uncle Tuku and moved more slowly; with each step he took his feet seemed to grow heavier until it was like heaving up two balls of lead. Once he kicked a little stone that had somehow got on to the fire-escape and it rattled down and down with a dreadful, earsplitting, heart-stopping sound. Ben stood still, half expecting all the windows in the house to blaze suddenly with light. None of them did.

3. On the first floor, the lower half of a window was open. He peered in. It was dark inside and the drawn curtains were heavy and thick, moving only very little in the light breeze. For a moment he waited, shivering, although the night was warm. Then he thought of Thomas, lying awake in the dark and worrying about his father, and pulled himself up, over the window-sill.

4. As his feet touched the floor inside the room, the light was switched on.
5. He stood, so rigid with fright that for a moment or two, though he heard voices, he had no idea what they were saying. He just closed his eyes and waited—waited for the curtains to be torn open, for the certain discovery. But . . . .

(From *On the Run* by Nina Bawden)

**Questions**

*Understanding the story*

1. Why would Ben go up the fire-escape stairs?
2. Which words suggest Ben did not know the layout of the house very well?
3. How would you explain why all the windows in the house did not open, as Ben expected, after "the earsplitting, heart-stopping sound"?
4. Why should Ben be shivering when the night was warm?
5. What kind of good news would Ben be bringing to Thomas?
6. Why did Ben not know what the voices were saying?
7. Which of the following is correct?
   (a) The night was bright and warm with a strong breeze.
   (b) The night was dark and cold with a slight breeze.
   (c) The night was dark and warm with a slight breeze.

*Cause and effect*

1. What caused Ben to move cautiously towards the house? *(paragraph 1)*
2. What caused Ben's heart to pound as he started to climb? *(paragraph 2)*
3. What was making the curtains move as Ben stood at the window? *(paragraph 3)*

*Figures of speech*

Write out and complete each of the following sentences using the phrases used in the passage.
1. In the dark night the windows were like . . . .   *(paragraph 1)*
2. Ben would go home as silent . . . .   *(paragraph 1)*
3. Ben's feet became heavy like . . . .   *(paragraph 2)*

Write out and complete each of the three sentences again. In the blanks use phrases other than those in the passage.

# 17 Fire!

1. "Stand back," was all Kizzy said.
2.     She meant to sprinkle a few drops but the tin was heavy. Petrol gushed out and, "Kizzy!" screamed Mary Jo as there was a bang and a flash of flame. Kizzy dropped the tin and jumped back as a sheet of fire came up. "How it didn't catch her face I don't know," said Elizabeth afterwards. In a moment there was what seemed a wall of fire with tongues reaching out towards the cottage; the thatch on the low eaves of the L caught at once, while the wind swept the fire upwards. Flames ran along the thatch and in a minute smoke began to come out of the upstairs windows. Chuff tore out of the house, his fur on end and leaped, clawing, up the hedge.
3.     The heat scorched the girls' faces and, "The wagon! The little wagon," screamed Elizabeth over the noise of the flames but, "Never mind the wagon," Kizzy shouted back. "Olivia . . . Miss Brooke, she's asleep in there." Before they could catch her, Kizzy had dodged round the flames and dived into the smoking cottage. Elizabeth screamed; Mary Jo began to sob, but Prudence was not Mrs Cuthbert's daughter for nothing. "Run, Beth," she ordered. "Run. Get Clem. Get men."
4. "Better . . . ring . . . fire brigade," choked Elizabeth.
5. "They would never believe children on bonfire night," Prue was cool, decisive. "Run!" and Elizabeth ran, dodging through the sitting-room which was not yet alight, but leaving the door open which fanned the flames; the sitting room began to fill with smoke but Prudence was still cool. "Mary Jo, come with me."
6. "In *there*?"
7. "We got to. Got to get 'em out. *Come on*. Don't chicken."
8.     As they came into the cottage, they heard faint cries. "We're coming," shouted Prue but she did not, like Kizzy,

dash straight up the stairs. She ran into the kitchen, found two glass cloths and held them under the tap. "Tie this over your mouth and nose," she commanded, giving one to Mary Jo. "Tie it tight. Now come."
9. "Up there?" Mary Jo quailed. "'S—moke."
10. "Course. Come on."

(From *The Diddakoi* by Rumer Godden)

## Questions

*Finding proof*

*What do you find in the passage to show that:*
(a) Prudence was the most calm of the four girls;
(b) Prudence was a good leader;
(c) Kizzy was liable to act quickly without thinking *(find two pieces of evidence which show this);*
(d) Mary Jo and Elizabeth were not very good at knowing what to do in an emergency such as this;
(e) Fire was a serious danger in this particular cottage?

*Main idea and supporting details*

*Paragraph 2 is mainly about* the fire attacking the cottage.
*Write out four supporting details:* (a) . . . (b) . . . (c) . . . (d) . . .

*Making inferences* (See page 66.)

*You are asked to make inferences in the following four questions. In each case explain why you gave the answer you did.*
1. Who or what was Chuff?
2. For what purpose might the girls have been using petrol?
3. Kizzy referred to one person (Miss Brooke) in the cottage. Later Prudence says, "Got to get 'em out". Why does Kizzy refer to one person and Prudence to more than one?
4. What would be the purpose of the wet glass cloths over their mouths and noses?

*Prediction* (See page 66.)

What do you think may have happened after Prudence said, "Course. Come on"?
*Write a few sentences to say what you think happened. (If you wish to check up to see whether you are correct, you must read the book.)*

# 18 Summarising

Often you may wish to write a summary of what you have read. You would try to include all the important points using as few words as possible.

To summarise a paragraph you would start by noting the main idea and the supporting details. This gives you an outline. (You have already practised this skill.)

Example: *A Bouncing Bomb* on page .
Main idea of paragraph 2   The bombing of targets in Germany.
Details:  (a)  planes flew out every day and every night
          (b)  attacked camps, railway yards and factories
          (c)  dropped bombs shaped like cigars with fins.

Let us try to write this out as a sentence of not more than 30 words. This will give us our summary.

Planes flew out every day and night to attack German targets such as camps, railway yards and factories by dropping bombs which were shaped like cigars and had fins.

1. *A Bouncing Bomb*
   Main idea of paragraph 4   How the bomb could be made to bounce.
   Details:  (a)  would be shaped like a dustbin
             (b)  made to spin backwards before dropping
             (c)  would bounce across the water.
   Try to make a summary *by writing out the points in the outline as a sentence of not more than 30 words.*

2. *Dam Busters* on page
   Main idea of paragraph 4   Improved defences of the Moehne Dam.
   Details:  (a)  pylons back from the wall of the dam
             (b)  cables with contact grenades strung down to the water
             (c)  anti-torpedo net near the wall.
   Make a summary *by writing out the outline as a sentence of about 30 words.*

3. Turn back to the outlines you already made in Unit 13. Write out each one as a summary.
   Try to write each summary as one sentence (if possible) and try to keep it down to about 30 words.

# 19 Escape from Colditz

1. They came upon a woodman's hut. The door was locked. By climbing on to the low roof and removing a few tiles they were able to drop inside. They made ready to spend the day there with suitable precautions. Wally detached the lock on the door and held it shut with a piece of string while Tubby cut out knots in the pine wood boards of the walls with his jack-knife providing spy holes in all directions. . . .

2. By midnight they were ready for the 'off'. The moon was shining brightly and had been helpful so far. Now, for the last lap, it would be a hindrance. It would help others to see them when they least wanted to be visible. There was a low ground mist on the other hand which would be useful if they chose to drop suddenly at an alarm.

3. They waited for a motor cycle patrol to pass with flashing headlamps, counted three minutes and crossed the road. Wally went about twenty yards in front of Tubby. They timed the crossing well, as a large cloud began to cover the face of the moon. They carried jack-knives in their sleeves. After twenty-five minutes of fast going, with the mist hiding them up to their waists, they approached the trees at the bottom of the hill. . . .

4. Suddenly a torch was flashed on Wally before he had time to drop, and there was a shout, "Halt! *Wer da?*". He approached the sentry in a roundabout way. Tubby had dropped and had not been seen. Wally forced the sentry to

turn with him as he advanced until his back was facing the direction where Tubby lay. The moon re-appeared, bathing the scene in an unearthly light. The sentry had not unslung his rifle. It was a good sign.

5.     Then, Wally distinguished the outline of his Tyrolean style cap, and his buttons gleamed showing up the Swiss cross. He looked beyond the sentry and saw the form of Tubby appearing out of the ground mist. He was much nearer than expected and Wally caught the glint of his knife as he moved noiselessly like a shadow. "Stop! Tubby, for God's sake!" he shouted over the guard's shoulder, "he's Swiss."

(From *Latter Days* by P. R. Reid)


## Questions

*Understanding the story*

1. Why do you think they were taking care when they were in the hut?
2. Why do you think Wally would take the lock off the door, especially when they did not wish to be disturbed?
3. Why was the mist to be more useful to them than moonlight?
4. For what are jack-knives used? For what were Wally and Tubby intending to use theirs if necessary?
5. Why would Wally and Tubby keep a distance apart as they walked towards the trees?
6. What mistake was Tubby making as he appeared out of the ground mist?

*Main ideas and supporting details*

*Copy down the main idea and add the supporting details.*
1. *Paragraph 1 is mainly about:* What they did at the woodman's hut.
   *Details:* (a) . . . , (b) . . . , (c) . . .
2. *Paragraph 2 is mainly about:* How the weather conditions would affect them.
   *Details:* (a) . . . , (b) . . . , (c) . . .

*Summaries*

1. *Combine the outline above for paragraph 1 into a sentence of roughly 30 words.*
2. *Do the same for paragraph 2.*

*Inferences* (See page 66.)

1. Why would they count three minutes after the patrol passed?
2. Why did Wally not run away when challenged by the sentry?
3. Wally was pleased to see that the sentry kept his rifle on his shoulder. What inference was Wally drawing?
4. What might Tubby have done if Wally had not shouted "He's Swiss!"?

*Exaggeration*

The moon gave an "unearthly light". Why would it appear so bright to Wally as he approached the sentry?

*Context clues* (See page 58.)

*Match each word in Column 1 with its meaning in Column 2. Look again at each word in Column 1 in the passage and look for clues to its meaning.*

| Column 1 | Column 2 |
| --- | --- |
| precautions *(paragraph 1)* | make out |
| hindrance *(paragraph 2)* | soldier on guard |
| visible *(paragraph 2)* | care taken beforehand |
| sentry *(paragraph 4)* | obstacle |
| distinguished *(paragraph 5)* | in view |

*Predicting outcomes* (See page 66.)

*Write a short story suggesting what happened next.*

# 20 River Rescue

1. But James was threshing with his arms wildly just out of Maria's reach. She leaned dangerously over the gunwales as Mr Copplestone tried to bring the boat near him. He was near the rushes at the edge of the river now, but as his eyes were tight shut in his panic there was no chance that he would have the sense to try to scramble out that way. "Oh, thank goodness, there are two men coming up on the bank," panted Maria, looking up for a moment. The men took in the situation at a glance, one of them lay on the bank while the other held him firm, and James was hauled on to dry earth.
2. "Oh, thank you," said Maria fervently.
3. "Shake him hard," said Mr Copplestone grimly to the two men, "until I can bring the boat into position to take on this monstrous child. Gentlemen, we are very much obliged to you."

4. James was not at all ashamed of himself when he climbed back into the boat. His hair was plastered in red streaks over his face, his clothes dripped into the bottom of the boat, while he talked excitedly of how cool it had been in the water, and how it had been the best part of the whole afternoon.
5. "Don't be so silly, James," said Joshua with exasperation, "you were absolutely terrified, shrieking and waving your arms about."
6. "That was because I was enjoying it so much. And of course I had to pretend I was frightened to make it more exciting."
7. "Why on earth didn't we leave him in the river?" said Thomas. "And have you thought of what you're going to say to Mamma when she sees you all wet? She'll never let you go near a river again."
8. "I'll dry by the time I get home."
9. "Oh, no, you won't," said Joshua. "Thomas, we'll have to try and keep it from Mamma. Perhaps we could dry his things in the attic without anybody finding out."
10. On the way from Bardwell Road to Canterbury Lane, James, with squelching noises coming from his sodden boots, marched between his two brothers, with Mr Copplestone in front and Maria behind him to try to hide him.

(From *The Warden's Niece* by Gillan Avery)

## Questions

*Context clues* (See page 58.)

*Study these words as used in the passage. Find clues to the meanings. Which is the meaning (a), (b), or (c)?*

1. panic *(paragraph 1)* (a) sudden great fear (b) amusement (c) anger
2. fervently *(paragraph 2)* (a) quietly (b) sadly (c) eagerly
3. monstrous *(paragraph 3)* (a) small (b) horrible (c) clever
4. exasperation *(paragraph 5)* (a) sadness (b) great anger (c) pleasure
5. shrieking *(paragraph 5)* (a) screaming (b) diving (c) jumping

*Check with your dictionary to see if you have chosen correctly.*

*Understanding the story*

1. James said he was pretending to be frightened. Joshua said James was terror-stricken. Which does paragraph 1 suggest was correct? Which phrases suggest this?
2. "The men took in the situation at a glance." What does this mean? What was the situation?
3. Suggest two reasons why James should have been ashamed of himself.
4. Who seems to have been most friendly to James
 (a) Mr Copplestone, (b) Maria, (c) Joshua, (d) Thomas? Why do you think so?
5. In spite of being annoyed with James, how do all four still show their friendship towards him?


*Making inferences* (See page 66.)

*Find clues which suggest:* (a) Maria might have been quite a brave girl.
(b) James often got himself into trouble.
(c) Mamma tended to worry about the children.


*Main ideas and details*

*Complete the following outlines. (Copy what you are given and write in missing details and the missing main idea.)*

*Paragraph 5 is mainly about:* What Joshua thought about James in the water.
*Details:* (a) . . . , (b) . . .

*Paragraph 6 is mainly about:* . . .
*Details:* (a) . . . , (b) Pretended to be frightened.


*Fact and opinion* (See page 72.)

*Which of the following are statements of fact and which are statements of opinion?*
1. James was a monstrous child.
2. James walked between his two brothers on the way home.
3. There were rushes at the edge of the river.

# 21 Sequence and Instructions

It is important to understand the order of events we are reading about. Very often writers record events in a different order from that in which they happened.

*Example:* Julie was able to tell her friends the story at school that day because she had been reading the book before she got up in the morning.

The events are recorded in this order:
(a) Julie told the story.  (b) Julie read the book.  (c) Julie got up.
Although they are told in the order (a), (b), (c), they happened in the order (b), (c), (a).

1. The events in the paragraph below are told in this order:
   (a) Andrew arrived at the gates   (b) Mr Jones, the watchman, went away   (c) Mr Jones wrote a message   (d) Andrew cycled towards Dean Park   (e) Andrew read the message
   *Write them out in the order they happened. The first one is (c).*

   By the time Andrew arrived at the gates, Mr Jones, the night-watchman, had gone, but before leaving Mr Jones had written a message on the board beside the window. Andrew cycled away towards Dean Park as soon as he had read the message.

2. *Put the following instructions in the correct order.*
   *To wash a car*
   (a)   Wash the car.
   (b)   Fill a pail with water and add detergent.
   (c)   Finally dry the car carefully with a chamois cloth.
   (d)   Rinse the soap off with clean water.
   (e)   Refill the pail with clean water only.

# 22 Paper Hats

Many kinds of paper hats, from paper cut out in a circle or a square, may be made up for parties and games.

*Coolie Hat*

*Follow the instructions below to make a coolie hat*
1. Cut out a square of thick paper and mark the centre (22 cms × 22 cms).
2. Use your compasses to draw a circle of radius 10 cm on the square of paper.
3. Cut out the circle.
4. Draw a radius of your circle.
5. Mark off a section like the one in Diagram (c).
6. Cut out the section you have marked off.
7. Mark off another section the same size and shade it in.
8. Gum the shaded section.
9. Pull the circular shape together to form a hat.
10. Overlap on the gummed section and stick together.
11. Secure with a small strip of sellotape.

*Below we see five stages* (a), (b), (c), (d), (e) *in the development of the making of the coolie hat. Which instruction had just been completed at each stage?*

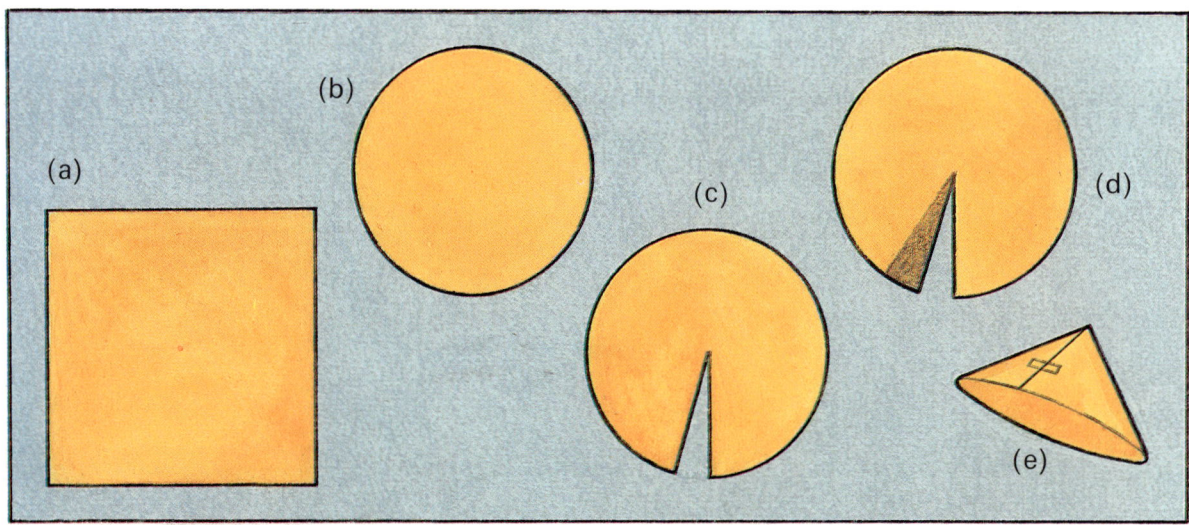

48

*Sombrero Hat*

*Try to make a sombrero hat. Follow the instructions given. Study the diagrams. Write out what you think the missing instructions should be.*

1. Cut out a square of thick paper (30 cm × 30 cm) and mark the centre.
2. Use your compasses to (a) draw a circle of radius 14 cm. and (b) draw an inner circle of radius 10 cm.
3. . . .
4. . . .
5. Mark off a section the same size as in Diagram 6.
6. . . .
7. . . .
8. Gum the shaded section.
9. . . .
10. Fold over along the inner circle for the turn up.
11. Reinforce join with gummed paper or sticky tape.
12. . . .

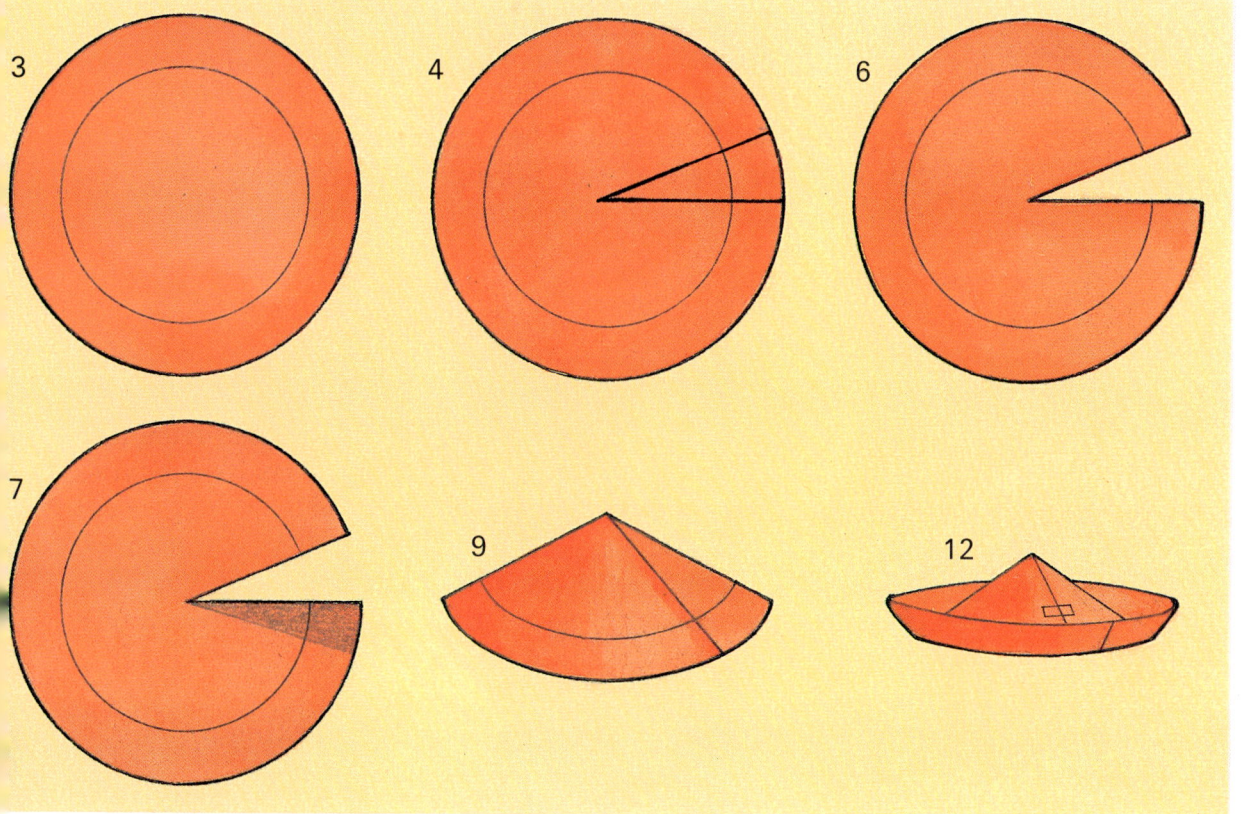

# 23 Into the Witch's Lair

1. Vernon and Jess, meanwhile, went very slowly on towards the bare patch in front of the hut. Jess was so frightened that she found it hard to put one foot before the other, for now they knew Biddy was some kind of witch, and Biddy had warned her and Frank to keep away. Vernon, Jess suspected, was almost as frightened as she was. It showed when he tried to make her go first between the petrol-drums, and it showed again when the cockerel flew up to the roof. Both of them ducked and put one arm up. Jess nearly ran away, only Vernon caught her coat and would not let her go.

2. Biddy did not seem to be there. Jess hoped she was out shopping, or something. She had often seen Biddy out shopping, with a string bag, all stooped over, peering through her glasses and taking big, irregular, swooping steps. Jess prayed she was doing it now. Vernon fidgeted and seemed to get over being frightened.

3. "I think she's out," Jess whispered.

4. "Shall we see?" Vernon asked, with a sideways sort of grin at her. Before Jess could stop him, he picked up a stick and hammered at a petrol-drum with it.

5. A hen squawked. The cat darted out of another drum and ran crouching into the hut. It was so fuggy that the echoes died quickly, as if someone had dropped a blanket over Jess's ears. She and Vernon stood in deep silence, until they heard a small shuffling inside the hut. Jess gasped. Vernon's eyes blinked whitely over at her. Then Biddy Iremonger came ambling cheerfully out through the door, still wearing her sack.

6. "Yes?" she said merrily. "Somebody knocking for me?"

7. "Me," said Vernon. "Us."

8. "Ah, good morning," said Biddy. "Vernon Wilkins, isn't

it?" She took no notice of Jess at all. "Now what do you want, young man?"

9. "Please," Vernon answered politely, "I would like to buy back the tooth Buster Knell gave you. How much is it, please?"

10. Biddy put her glasses straight with a big purple hand and peered at Vernon through them.

(From *Wilkins' Tooth* by Diana Wynne Jones)

## Questions

*Context clues* (See page 51.)

*Find the word in the passage which means:*
(a) moved restlessly *(paragraph 2)*; (b) gave a harsh cry *(paragraph 5)*; (c) stuffy *(paragraph 5)*; (d) moving along easily and gently *(paragraph 5)*.

*Understanding the story*

1. (a) Why were Vernon and Jess so frightened? (b) Which one was the more afraid?
2. Why do you think Vernon did not allow Jess to run away?
3. In your own words how would you describe Biddy? What would make her particularly frightening?
4. Give two reasons why you think Vernon spoke to Biddy in such a humble and good-mannered way.

*Finding proof*

1. What proves that they were frightened as they approached the hut?
2. What suggests that they were frightened when they heard the shuffling in the hut?

*Making inferences* (See page 66.)

1. Why would they hope that Biddy was out?
2. What might they have been intending to do if she was out?

*Prediction* (See page 66.)

What do you think happened next? *Write a few sentences to suggest what might have happened.*
*If you really want to find out you must read* Wilkins' Tooth *by Diana Wynne Jones.*

# 24 Trailing a Thief

1. Three of the scouts whom Gustav had posted along Trautenau Street now came tearing into Nicholas Square, beckoning frantically to the young detectives.
2. "Come on," shouted the Professor, and he, Emil, the two Mittlers, and Krumm tore off towards Kaiser Avenue as if they were trying to break the world record for the hundred yards. They slowed down as they approached the newspaper stand and came on more cautiously, as Gustav was making signs of some sort to them.
3. "Are we too late?" panted Emil.
4. "Don't be daft," Gustav whispered back. "If I say I'll do a thing, I do it properly."
5. Then they saw the thief standing on the pavement outside the cafe, looking about him as though he were in Switzerland, admiring the view. He bought an evening paper from the newsvendor and glanced at the headlines.
6. "It'll be a bit awkward if he comes this way," remarked Krumm. They were hiding behind the news-stand, but keeping a watchful eye on him. They were all agog with excitement. The thief went on reading his paper, and seemed to pay no attention to anything else.
7. "I believe he's squinting over the top of it to see if he's being watched," said the elder Mittler.
8. "Did he seem to look your way much while you were waiting?" the Professor asked Gustav.
9. "No, not once," Gustav replied. "He was too busy eating. You'd have thought he hadn't had a meal for days."
10. "Look out," cried Emil abruptly.
11. The man was folding up his paper. He gave a quick glance at the passers-by and hailed a taxi. It drew up, and he got in and slammed the door. By that time the boys had also hailed a taxi, and Gustav said to the driver,
12. "Follow that taxi which is just turning into Prague Place, please, but don't let the man inside it see he's being tailed."

(From *Emil and the Detectives* by Erich Kästner)

## Questions

*Context clues*
(See page 58.)

Study each word as used in the story and decide which of the three suggestions (a), (b) or (c) is the meaning.

beckoning *(paragraph 1)* (a) looking  (b) smiling  (c) making a sign with the head or hand.

frantically *(paragraph 1)* (a) loudly  (b) desperately  (c) slowly
abruptly *(paragraph 10)* (a) suddenly  (b) quietly  (c) sadly

*Understanding the story*

1. What was making the young detectives look as if they were trying to break the world record for the hundred yards? Why?
2. Who seemed to be the chief of the detectives?
3. Emil wondered if they were late, but what would Gustav have been trying to convey by his signs?
4. What would suggest that the thief did not know he was being followed when he was outside the cafe?
5. Which words suggest he was unworried as he read the paper?
6. What else indicates the thief was not worried about being followed?
7. Why should Emil cry out *abruptly*?

*Predicting outcomes* (See page 66.)

Write a few sentences to suggest how the story might have ended.

# 25 Arctic Explorers

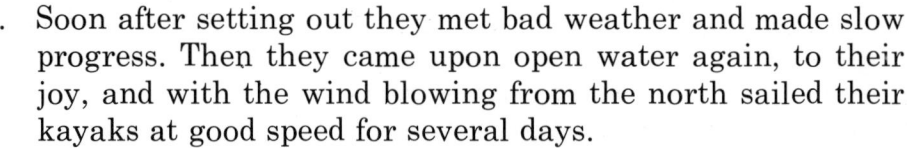

1. Soon after setting out they met bad weather and made slow progress. Then they came upon open water again, to their joy, and with the wind blowing from the north sailed their kayaks at good speed for several days.

2. One evening they put in to the edge of the ice to stretch their legs, being stiff from sitting in the kayaks all day. They went up to a small hill and Johansen, looking back, suddenly shouted that the kayaks were adrift—the rope, made of walrus hide, had given way. All they possessed was on board; they had not even a knife with them. Nansen threw off some clothing and dived into the icy water. He swam fast but the kayaks, lashed together, were drifting rapidly. Nansen felt his arms and legs growing numb, and thought that whether he sank or turned back without the kayaks, the result would be the same. These were the worst moments he ever lived through, he afterwards admitted. At last he reached the kayaks and was able to grasp one of the skis lying across the stern, then struggled to get aboard. By then he was so stiff with cold that he had great difficulty in paddling. He was shivering all over and the gusts of wind went right through his wet woollen shirt.

3. Amazingly, when he saw two auks on the water he got hold of his gun and shot them. Johansen, worried as he walked agitatedly up and down on the ice, heard the shots and thought there had been an accident; then when he saw Nansen pick up the birds he thought his friend had gone out of his mind. When Nansen reached the shore, Johansen had to undress him and pack him into the sleeping-bag to thaw out, then cooked the auks for supper.

4. Three days later they thought they heard a dog barking. Nansen went on, leaving Johansen to mind the kayaks.

5. "It was with a strange mixture of feelings," Nansen wrote later, "that I made my way in towards land. Suddenly I thought I heard a shout from a human voice, a strange voice, the first for three years. Soon ... I saw a dark form moving among the ridges of ice farther in. It was a dog; but farther off came another figure, and that was a man. Who was it?"

(Adapted from *Famous Arctic Adventures* by Len Ortzen)

## Questions

*Understanding the passage*

1. Were Nansen and Johansen on their own or with others?
2. Were they travelling in a northerly or southerly direction?
3. What time of year do you think it was in the Arctic? Summer or Winter? Why do you think so?
4. Nansen thought "the result would be the same". What would the result be?
5. What suggests that they had very little food?
6. How long, at least, had they been on the expedition together?

*Cause and effect*

*In this section write each answer for (a) to (e) in a sentence using the word* because *in each one.*
What was the reason for:
(a) their being able to travel at a fast rate
(b) their going ashore on the ice
(c) Nansen throwing off his clothes before swimming
(d) Johansen being worried as he walked about on the ice
(e) Johansen being left to look after the kayaks *(paragraph 4)*

*Making inferences* (See page 66.)

1. What kind of bad weather might there have been?
2. What might have caused the rope to give way?

*Fact and opinion*

*Decide from your reading of the passage whether each of the following is a statement of fact* or *of opinion. If you write* opinion *say why.*
1. Nansen shot two birds.
2. Nansen was out of his mind when he shot the auks.
3. Food was becoming short.
4. Johansen heard shots.

*Alphabetical order*

*Find the word in the passage which means:* (a) shaking with cold *(paragraph 2),* (b) losing feeling because of the cold *(paragraph 2),* (c) sudden blaste *(paragraph 2),* (d) mishap *(paragraph 3),* (e) become warmer *(paragraph 3).*
*Write out the five words you found in the order you would find them in a dictionary.*

# 26 The Moving Toffee-Bar

1. As she leant forward over the big table in the centre of the classroom to push the folders across it, something climbed out of her pocket and landed with a soft *clump* on the table. Gwinny craned her head round. She stared, frozen and bent over. It was the toffee-bar she had borrowed from Johnny, complete with its white and yellow wrapper. And it was crawling across the table in a slow, deliberate way, as if it knew where it was going.
2. "No, stop! Come back!" Gwinny said to it. She felt all guilty. The toffee-bar was alive, and she had no doubt that it was the bottle Douglas spilt which had done it. She put down the folders, a little nervously. She was not exactly frightened. The toffee-bar was only four inches long and flat as a ruler. But, even so, if it was alive, it was not precisely a toffee-bar any longer.
3. The toffee-bar crawled steadily on until it came to a patch of sunlight in the middle of the table. There, it stopped and stretched and coiled itself this way and that with evident enjoyment.
4. "Oh, do come back!" Gwinny said to it.
5. But the toffee-bar took no notice. It stretched several times more, rather harder. Then, quite suddenly, the white and yellow paper split in two along the top of it. The toffee inside wriggled a little, and then it crawled out from the paper, a smooth yellow-brown strip.
6. "I'll have to catch you," Gwinny said firmly. She reached out, not quite so firmly, and tried to take hold of the toffee-bar. It must have seen her hand coming. Its brown body jack-knifed and leapt away from her fingers. In a flash, it had jumped off the table, wriggled over the floor, and gone to earth in a shelf of library books.

(From *The Ogre Downstairs* by Diana Wynne Jones)

## Questions

*Understanding the passage*

1. In what kind of a building do these events take place? Which clues tell you?
2. Why would it be natural for Gwinny to "stare, frozen and bent over"?
3. What did the contents of Douglas's bottle seem to be able to do?
4. Why would the toffee-bar not be exactly "a toffee-bar any longer"?
5. For what reasons do you think the toffee-bar went to the sunlit patch?
6. What evidence is there that the toffee-bar could see?
7. What did the toffee-bar seem to be trying to do when Gwinny tried to catch it?

*Figurative language*

The writer uses figurative language to make the scene more exciting and interesting.

1. What does she really mean when she says Gwinny was frozen?
2. She does not simply say the toffee-bar was flat. With what does she compare it? This makes us think of it as what else besides flat?
3. A jack-knife is a strong clasp knife which springs shut. What does the writer mean when she says the toffee-bar jack-knifed?
4. "In a flash it had jumped off the table." Write out what this sentence means in your own words.
5. The toffee-bar had "gone to earth". But it was not down on any earth. What does this expression mean?

# 27 Context Clues

When you come across a word such as *hard* in a sentence, you will usually be able to tell what it means by reading the full sentence.

A. *Below are three sentences. Each sentence contains the word* hard *and it means something different each time. Read each sentence. Look at the word* hard *in it.*
   (a) In which sentence does it mean *solid, firm?*
   (b) Now decide in which sentence hard means *not easy to understand.*
   (c) Where does hard mean *having no kind feelings?*

1. Thomas said he could not answer these hard questions.
2. Anne was hard. She would not help Grace or lend her any money.
3. The ice was as hard as a rock.

*For each of the following sentences in groups B and C decide the meaning of the word underlined which fits the sentence best.*

B.  1. Donald had never played any <u>game</u> in the stadium.
    2. Mr Roberts did not take his gun as he thought there would be no <u>game</u> at that time of year.
    3. The wrestler was very <u>game</u>. He kept getting up again.

    (a) plucky
    (b) a sport of any kind
    (c) wild animals and birds hunted for sport

C.  1. The train was signalled to stop because of a frozen <u>point</u>.
    2. Francis had to note the <u>point</u> at which the metal melted.
    3. The archer was injured by the <u>point</u> of an enemy spear.

    (a) sharp end
    (b) exact moment
    (c) joining of railway lines

D. *Clues in the sentence or paragraph often help you to recognise the meaning of a word. Decide from clues what is the meaning of each word underlined. Write down (a), (b) or (c).*

1. Mr Williams said it would be better to build a new house altogether than to spend a lot of money renewing the dilapidated house he had been left in his uncle's will.
   *dilapidated:* (a) stone-built, (b) falling to pieces, needing repairs, (c) isolated.

2. The policeman knew something was wrong when he saw Frank disappear over the bank and David begin to gesticulate furiously.

   *gesticulate:* (a) walk about, (b) cheer, (c) wave arms and hands about in excitement.

3. The plants required a great deal of water. It was necessary to saturate them every day.

   *saturate:* (a) to weed, (b) to soak thoroughly, (c) to move to another place.

E. *Look for clues to help you to guess the meaning of each word underlined. Write down the meaning you think would suit and then check with your dictionary to see if you are correct.*

At night the rooms were illuminated by candles which could only be bought at extortionate prices. The very rich people could afford them but others had no proper light in their rooms at all.

# 28 Unhappy Christmas

1. It got dark about two o'clock in the loft, but we stayed where we were because we knew it wouldn't be dark outside. We thought we'd better give it till four.
2. They had the wireless on loud in the house, and we kept track of the time by that. We heard Forces' Favourites and carol singing and a kids' party going on in a hospital somewhere. Then they did the round-the-world hook-up they do every Christmas, and we heard what everybody round the world had for their Christmas dinner. They had turkey and goose and plum pudding. We had mince pies for ours. They'd got a bit mashed in Soldier's pocket, but we ate them and had a look to see if there was anything else to eat, carrots or turnips or anything, but there wasn't. So we sat and heard what they had round the world.
3. A gale of wind blew up through the trap door and we huddled as far from it as we could, half frozen and ravenously hungry.
4. We didn't talk much. There wasn't much to talk about. We knew we had to keep away from people—which meant no lifts and no taxis—and that we had about seven miles to cover to Little Gippings. We'd have to cover them on foot, in the dark. With the snow, and my leg, we couldn't do more than a mile and a half an hour. So if we got out of the loft at four we ought to get there by nine.
5. It wasn't much of a prospect. We sat and thought about it, in the icy blast from the trapdoor, and waited for the pips on the wireless to tell us when it was four and time to go.
6. A bit of traffic passed on the main road while we waited, and once during the afternoon someone came out of the house and shovelled coal. That was about all that happened.
7. I tried to sleep, huddled up with my arms round my legs and my chin on my knees, and I must have succeeded, because the next thing I knew, Soldier was shaking me, and it was time.

(From *Run for your Life* by David Lene)

## Questions

*Context clues*

1. By spotting clues in the passage, find the word which means  (a) radio *(paragraph 2)*,  (b) exceedingly hungry *(paragraph 3)*,  (c) outlook *(paragraph 5)*.
2. What kind of a loft was it? Which clues tell you?
3. How do you know it was afternoon and not night-time?
4. How do you know that the writer was very tired?

*Cause and effect*

1. Why would they not wish to see anyone?
2. What might have been the result if they had tried to get a lift?
3. What caused their slow progress (1.5 miles an hour)?
4. For what reason did they plan to wait two hours after it was dark in the loft?
5. What, apart from the shortage of food, might have made them feel so terribly hungry?

*What do you think?*

1. Why do you think they were hiding?
2. Why do you think that they did not seek help from the people in the house?

*Predicting outcomes* (See page 66).

Suggest what might have happened to them between 4 o'clock and 9 o'clock.

# 29 Eskimos Today

1. If you were going to visit Eskimo country, you might fly to Frobisher and there stay in its pleasant hotel built for visitors just like you. In this small town you would have your first encounter with Eskimos. Nearly 2000 of these friendly people live there.

2. On your holiday you would be unlikely to travel by husky-drawn sledge. That is now the transport of the minority. If you go by sledge at all, it would most probably be a modern motor sledge. Your long journeys would be by plane and not by sea. Ships no longer need to try to force their way through the ice. And if you wished to see the North Pole you could become one of the many who have flown over it.

3. Some Eskimos do live a hard life in igloos. But it might come as a surprise to learn that the number of such people has fallen dramatically since 1950. The Canadian government helped to build villages where many now live in modern huts. They buy and sell in their own stores and draw family allowances for their children and send them to the nearby school. Many others live in the new small towns built beside the radar stations which were set up in the Arctic to give early warning of attack on America by plane or missile. In Frobisher you can see town dwellers enjoying modern houses with kitchens, oil fires and radios. A far cry indeed from the Eskimos of the time of Nansen and Johansen.

4. In those days many hunted for the animals whose furs were so valuable. Although still highly prized, they are not now Eskimos' only source of wealth. In the Canadian Arctic nickel, petroleum and copper have been discovered. These finds soon meant that miners and machine operators were needed. Many Eskimos learned such trades from the early miners and prospectors who rushed there.

5. For many Eskimos life has become very much easier. Thousands have never learned the skills which enabled people in olden days to survive severe cold, food shortages and spells of isolation. Early explorers learned from the Eskimos how to survive. How many Eskimos could now survive themselves, let alone teach anyone else?

**Questions**

*Context clues*

*Find the word in the passage which means:*
(a) meeting *(paragraph 1)*, (b) number less than half *(paragraph 2)*,
(c) very sharply *(paragraph 3)*, (d) living away from other people *(paragraph 5)*.

*Understanding the story:*

*Find proof that:*
1. Frobisher has an airport, hotel and nearly 2000 Eskimo inhabitants.
2. Few ships now carry goods and people in the Canadian Arctic.
3. Many people have flown over the Pole.
4. Many Eskimos now have modern housing.
5. Minerals have been found in the Arctic.

*Main ideas and supporting details*

*Which paragraph deals mainly with:*
1. How modern Eskimos live
2. Forms of transport
3. How Eskimos can earn their living. (What sorts of jobs can they get?)

*Add supporting details for each of the three paragraphs.*

*Cause and effect*

1. Why have so many Eskimos abandoned life in igloos?
2. What has caused ships to become less important?
3. What would have caused miners and prospectors to rush to the Canadian Arctic?

*Make up your own questions*

1. Which questions could be answered by paragraph 1?
2. Paragraph 5 ends in a question. Write out two questions which could be answered from the rest of the paragraph.

*Summary*

You have already made an outline of paragraph 2. Write it out in sentence form to make a summary.

# 30 A Hard and Lonely Life

1. Would you really like to be a cowboy? The life seems glamorous and full of fun when we watch many western films made over the years. But in the days of the old west, and even today, the life of the cowboy was hard, lonely, often boring, and sometimes dangerous.

2. As Americans moved out into the wide open spaces of the west in the mid-1800s, cattle-raising became one of the main activities. The cattle might be spread out over many miles of ranchland. Men were needed to take care of them, to round up strays, and to bring the herd to market. These men came to be called cowhands, or cowboys.

3. Cowboys, then and now, often "ride herd" for days or weeks at a time. Normally, they live in bunkhouses on the ranch, but when out on the range, they quite often sleep under the stars, or in tents. They get their meals, then, from a chuckwagon, a sort of travelling kitchen on wheels.

4. Although many people think of cowboys as looking something like John Wayne, they come in all sizes, shapes, and even colours. Many Negroes, and even Japanese and Chinese, worked as cowboys in the west.

5. The cowboys wear distinctive outfits and carry their "six guns". (Perhaps you have your cowboy suit and guns.) They sing famous songs, some of which you will know. Books and films often make them seem brave men living a life that is one great whirl of excitement. No wonder they came to be looked on as heroes all over the world.

(Adapted from *United States of America* by John Bear)

## Questions

*Context clues*

*Find the word which means:* (a) exciting *(paragraph 1),* (b) jobs *(paragraph 2),* (c) different from others *(paragraph 5).*

*Understanding the passage*

1. What, according to the writer, is similar in the life of a cowboy today and in the life of a cowboy of days long ago?
2. What was the main occupation for Americans as they moved west last century?
3. What made the cowboy's life so hard?
4. What in the passage proves that people other than Americans became cowboys?
5. What made so many people look upon cowboys as heroes?

*Fact and opinion* (See page 72.)

*Is each of the following a statement of* fact *or of* opinion? *(Could proof be found for the statement, or is the statement just the opinion of one or more persons?)*

1. The cowboy's life is full of fun.
2. The cowboy's life is a hard one.
3. Chinese have worked as cowboys.
4. Cowboys sometimes sleep in tents.

*Alphabetical order*

*Write the following words in alphabetical order:*
   Negroes   Japanese   Chinese   cowboy   ranch   market

# 31 Inferences and Predicting Outcomes

When you are reading your mind understands more than your eyes actually see.

A. 1. *What can you tell about:*

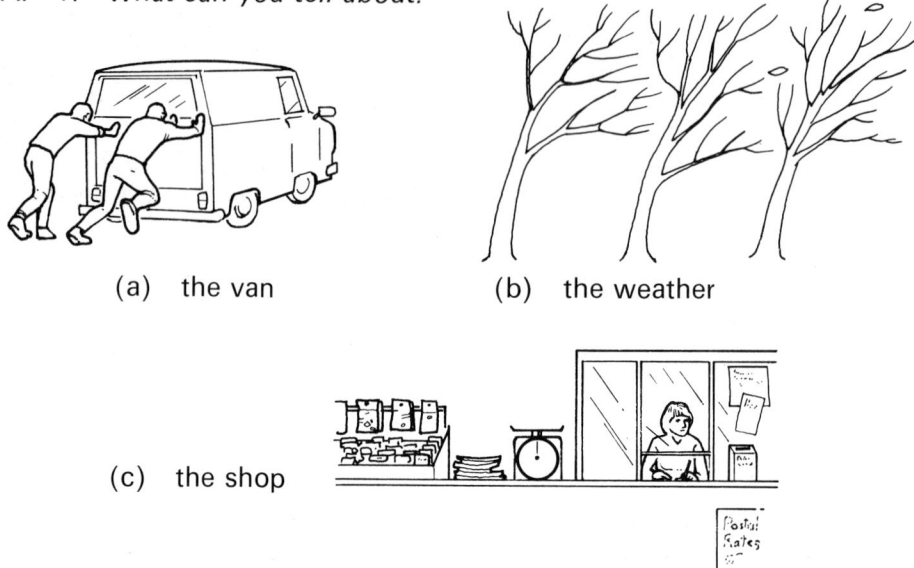

(a) the van

(b) the weather

(c) the shop

2. *What do you think is the occupation of the person underlined in each of the following?*

(a) <u>Jean</u> looked over the hastily scribbled notes of Mr Arthur and then sat down at her typewriter.

(b) <u>Bill</u> came out of his van and lifted his ladder, sponges, and cloths.

(c) <u>Mary</u> unlocked the second lock on the door and allowed the other employees to enter. When they had all taken their places at the counter she unlocked the night safe.

B. *Read each paragraph and answer the questions below it.*

1. Mr Willis, the chauffeur, held open the door as June climbed into the back of her father's new, gleaming Rolls Royce. Her father sat beside her and asked Mr Willis to

drive slowly because they were early. As they approached the church the crowd moved forward smiling and cheering. The photographer came to greet them.

(a) Why do you think they would be going to church?
(b) Would you think June's father might be fairly rich or very poor? Why?

2. Captain Brown ordered his crew to cut away the nets and let them sink. The engines roared at full speed as he headed out to sea. Approaching at high speed was the patrol vessel which prevented fishing within the three mile limit.

*What inference do you draw from each of the following?*
(a) Captain Brown allowed his nets to sink.
(b) He headed his ship out to sea.
(c) The patrol vessel approached at high speed.
*Can you guess the outcome? Write a few sentences to say what you think happened next.*

3. George radioed to William that his fuel indicator was reaching zero with 50 kilometres still to travel. William sounded the alarm for fire engines and ambulances to stand by.

(a) How was George travelling?
(b) What might William's job have been?
(c) Write three sentences to suggest what might have happened.

*You have made many inferences and predictions. Some will be correct and perhaps others will be wrong. Discuss with other pupils or with your teacher which ideas you like best.*

# 32 Survivors

1. Sturt Plain, where the aircraft had crashed, is in the centre of the Northern Territory. It is roughly the size of England and Wales combined; but instead of some 45 000 000 inhabitants, it has roughly 4 500, and instead of some 200 000 roads, it has two, of which one is a fair-weather stock route. Most of the inhabitants are grouped round three or four small towns—Tennant Creek, Hooker Creek, and Daly Waters—which means that the rest of the area is virtually uninhabited. The Plain is fourteen hundred miles from Adelaide and is not a good place to be lost in.

2. Had they known enough to weigh up their chances, the children would have realized their only hope was to stay beside the wrecked plane; to rely on rescue from the air. But this never occurred to them. Adelaide was somewhere to the south. So southward they started to walk.

3. The girl worked things out quietly, sensibly—she wasn't the sort to get into a panic. The sun had risen there: on the

left of the gully: so that would be east. South, then, must be straight ahead; down-stream. That was lucky. Perhaps they'd be able to follow the creek all the way to the sea; all the way to Adelaide. She knotted the four corners of Peter's handkerchief, dipped it in the water, and draped it over his head—for already the sun was uncomfortably hot.

4. "Come on, Peter," she said, "let's go."
5. She led the way down the gully.
6. At first the going was easy. Close to the stream, rocks of granite and quartz provided safe footing; and the trees, sprouting from every pocket of clay, were thick enough to give a welcome shade, but not so thick that they hindered progress. Mary pushed steadily on.

(From *Walkabout* by James Vance Marshall)

## Questions

*Reading for details*

*You will have to read much more slowly and much more carefully to find whether each of the following sentences is* True *or* False *or whether the passage* Doesn't Tell.

1. Northern Territory is roughly as big as England and Wales.
2. Nearly as many people live in Northern Territory as live in England and Wales.
3. Tennant Creek is a larger town than Daly Waters.
4. A plane was already looking for the children when they started to walk.
5. Peter worked out the direction they should travel.
6. They were glad to have the trees for shade.

*Following directions on a map*

1. If the sun had risen on Mary's left, in which direction would she be facing? Was her calculation correct?
2. In what direction does Adelaide lie from where they landed? Was Mary correct?

*Predicting outcomes*

What do you think happened to Peter and Mary?

# 33 Tyke on the Roof

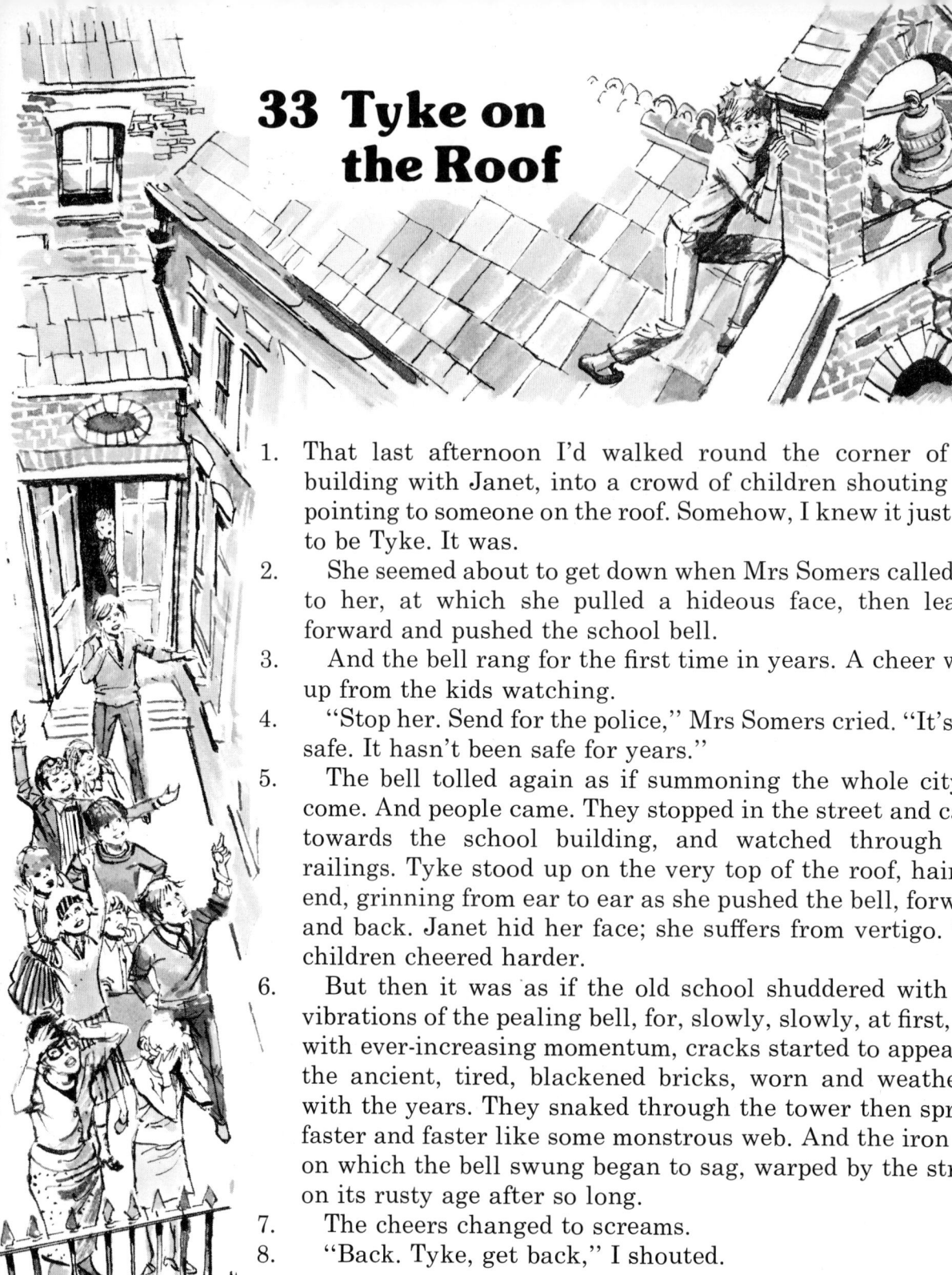

1. That last afternoon I'd walked round the corner of the building with Janet, into a crowd of children shouting and pointing to someone on the roof. Somehow, I knew it just had to be Tyke. It was.
2. She seemed about to get down when Mrs Somers called out to her, at which she pulled a hideous face, then leaned forward and pushed the school bell.
3. And the bell rang for the first time in years. A cheer went up from the kids watching.
4. "Stop her. Send for the police," Mrs Somers cried. "It's not safe. It hasn't been safe for years."
5. The bell tolled again as if summoning the whole city to come. And people came. They stopped in the street and came towards the school building, and watched through the railings. Tyke stood up on the very top of the roof, hair on end, grinning from ear to ear as she pushed the bell, forward and back. Janet hid her face; she suffers from vertigo. The children cheered harder.
6. But then it was as if the old school shuddered with the vibrations of the pealing bell, for, slowly, slowly, at first, but with ever-increasing momentum, cracks started to appear in the ancient, tired, blackened bricks, worn and weathered with the years. They snaked through the tower then spread faster and faster like some monstrous web. And the iron bar on which the bell swung began to sag, warped by the strain on its rusty age after so long.
7. The cheers changed to screams.
8. "Back. Tyke, get back," I shouted.

(From *The Turbulent Term of Tyke Tiler* by Gene Kemp)

**Questions**

*Context clues*

Use clues in the passage to help you to find the word which means:
(a) frightful, horrible *(paragraph 2)*, (b) sending for *(paragraph 5)*,
(c) giddiness *(paragraph 5)*, (d) shaking *(paragraph 6)*,
(e) force *(paragraph 6)*, (f) twisted out of shape *(paragraph 6)*.

*Understanding the story*

1. Why do you think Tyke did not come down when Mrs Somers asked?
2. What would Mrs Somers hope the police might do?
3. In what way would you say that Tyke and Janet were unlike?
4. What can you tell from the story about: (a) the age of the building, and (b) the state of the building?

*Making inferences*

1. The writer says he knew that "it just had to be Tyke". What does this suggest to you about Tyke?
2. Which of the following do you think might apply to Tyke:
   (a) easily frightened, (b) dare-devil, (c) well known for pranks?
3. Why do you think the onlooking children cheered?

*Cause and effect*

1. What caused the school to shudder?
2. What caused the cheers to turn to screams?

*Figurative language*

1. What is the pattern of cracks compared to? Would you say this is a good or a bad comparison? Why?
2. The cracks *snaked* through the tower. Why is *snaked* a good word to describe the cracks opening up?
3. Sometimes writers use exaggeration when they write. What does the writer mean when he says:
   (a) Tyke was *grinning from ear to ear*, and (b) She stood up *hair on end*?

# 34 Fact and Opinion

A lot of the print we see every day is trying to persuade us (for example: *"Buy . . ."*). We must be able to sort out facts and opinions.

A. An opinion is what a person, or more than one person, thinks about something, e.g. *The houses in our street are attractive.* This is an opinion. Your opinion may be different. You may not find the houses attractive.

*Answer each of the following questions. Your answer will be your opinion. It is not necessarily true or untrue. It is your point of view.*

1. Who is the most handsome pop star you have seen?
2. What is the best TV programme?
3. What is the best time of year to go away for a holiday?
4. Which author writes the most exciting books for readers of your age?

*Compare your answers with those of your friends. Different people have different opinions. When we say something is* best *we are often expressing an opinion.*

B. *Let us now try to recognise the difference between* fact *and* opinion. *There are five sentences below. Two are facts and three are opinions. Which are which?*

1. Edinburgh is the capital of Scotland.
2. Edinburgh is the finest city in the world.
3. Many tourists come to Edinburgh every year.
4. Edinburgh is more beautiful than any other place in Scotland.
5. The Palace of Holyroodhouse is well worth a visit.

C. *Decide whether each sentence is* fact *or* opinion. *Number 1 to 5 in your book, and write* fact *or* opinion *for each sentence.*

1. The first electric train in England ran in 1890 on the City and South London Railway. 2. The carriages were small and each was designed to hold only 32 people. 3. I think it might have been much more fun to travel in one of them rather than in one of today's modern carriages. 4. It would have been much more exciting than going by stage coach. 5. But a journey by pony and trap would have been most enjoyable of all.

# 35 Bull Fighting

1. The sight of a fearless matador fighting a bull in a ring makes, for many people, a show well worth seeing. Others would view it with anger and disgust. In Spain it has for long been one of the most popular types of entertainment.

2. There are normally three parts of a bullfight. First, picadors annoy the bull by prodding it with long poles. Very soon they arouse the bull's instincts to defend itself. Next, as the bull tries to attack its enemies they drive three-centimetre barbs into its neck. In the meantime the matador watches how it reacts. Finally when he considers the time suitable he will come into the ring and make passes round the animal which is now raging and nearly crazy. His steps to avoid the bull are rather like those of a ballet dancer. He brings the show to an end by running it through with his sword, that is if he wins.

3. After the dead bull has been dragged out, another one is let loose in the ring and the next fight begins.

4. The earliest origins of bullfighting seem to be found in the worship of the ancient Persian god, Mithra. Pictures show him as a beautiful youth slaying a bull. As the worship of this god spread amongst Roman Emperors and soldiers, so did the practice of bullfighting. In the Middle Ages, Spanish aristocrats lanced bulls from horseback. In due course the sport was taken up by the lower classes. As they could not afford horses, they fought on foot. In this way the modern type of bullfighting began.

5. There are quite a number of people in Spain who do not like bullfights. In several countries groups of people have joined together to try to stop the killings for sport. They think that all blood sports should be banned. But for the present, bullfighting looks like being continued for years to come. The practice is a tradition which very many Spaniards hope will last for a long time.

(Adapted from *Spain, the Land and its Peoples*, *Macdonald Countries* series)

## Questions

*Context clues*

Using clues in the passage, find the word which means: (a) natural feelings *(paragraph 2)*, (b) beginnings *(paragraph 4)*, (c) nobles *(paragraph 4)*, (d) custom which is handed down *(paragraph 5)*.

*Main ideas*

Which paragraph deals mainly with?
1. Should bull fighting be stopped?
2. How bull fighting began and developed.
3. The three parts of a bull fight.

*Supporting details*

Copy down the main ideas headings and add three supporting details for each.
When you have finished you will have made an outline of each of three paragraphs.

*Summarising*

Refer to your outlines without looking at the passage. Combine each outline into a sentence of not more than 30 words.

*Are you able to read with very great care?*

According to the passage, is each of the following statements True or False or is it the case that the passage Doesn't Say?
1. People pay to watch bull fights.
2. Many picadors are injured in bull fights.
3. Bull fights became popular with the Romans.
4. Dead bulls are taken to butchers to be cut up for meat to be sold.
5. There are groups opposed to bull fighting.
6. The majority of Spaniards would now like to stop bull fighting.

*Whose opinion?*

Who would be most likely to hold the following opinions?
1. Bull fighting is a very good sport.
2. Bull fighting is a cruel sport and should be banned.
Which is your opinion? (1) or (2)? Why?

# 36 Paradurra Megalocephala Abyssinienses

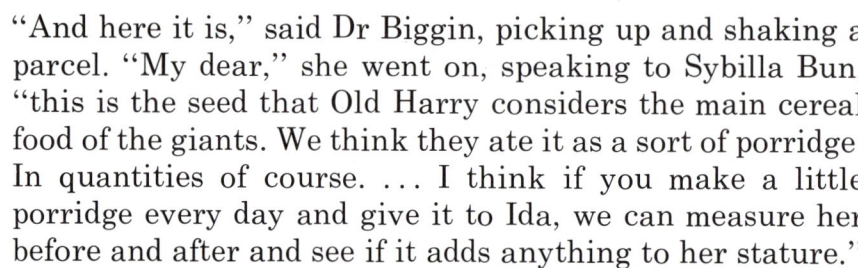

1. "And here it is," said Dr Biggin, picking up and shaking a parcel. "My dear," she went on, speaking to Sybilla Bun, "this is the seed that Old Harry considers the main cereal food of the giants. We think they ate it as a sort of porridge. In quantities of course. ... I think if you make a little porridge every day and give it to Ida, we can measure her before and after and see if it adds anything to her stature."

2. "Would it not be better," Sybilla said tactlessly, "if we gave it to Oskar, as he is growing so much anyway? You would get much more interesting results."

3. Dr Biggin was deeply affronted.

4. "You have no idea of scientific investigation at all, Sybilla. I specially chose Ida because she is not growing. For one thing, if she does grow it will be as near proof as we could get. For another thing she is much too small so we can afford to experiment with her. It would be an improvement. Whereas the effect on Oskar might be disastrous. He might shoot into a giant before the end of the holidays." ...

5. Miss Bun was a little hurt too. She lifted the lid off the coffee-pot and inhaled the aroma with closed eyes to restore herself. Then she said: "Well, that means that dear Oskar can have some nice real porridge. I don't imagine," she added, twitching her shoulders so that her beads rattled, "that the Ogru were good cooks." ...

6. "Now don't get upset, Sybilla. Old Harry has suggested bringing the Committee here for your cooking as much as for anything else."

7. Miss Bun was mollified. Smoked salmon, chicken Maryland with dry Hock, crepes Suzette, melon and ginger ice. . . .
8. "It would be nice," said Maud Biggin openly winking at the children, "if you could make us a kidney risotto with *Paradurra megalocephala abyssiniensis*. They would be interested."
9. Miss Bun grew crimson.
10. "I shall do no such thing, Maud. The most I shall do with your miserable grass seeds is a gruel for Ida. It is the domain of medicine, not of good eating. Good eating is an Art."
11. After breakfast Ida was solemnly measured, lying on the wooden floor so that she could not cheat by stretching.

(From *The River at Green Knowe* by Lucy M. Boston)

## Questions

*Context clues*

*Find the word in the story which means:* (a) thoughtlessly *(paragraph 2),* (b) insulted *(paragraph 3),* (c) smell *(paragraph 5),* (d) calmed down *(paragraph 7).*
Check your answers in your dictionary.

*Understanding the story*

1. What effect did Dr Biggin think eating the seed would have?
2. How was Dr Biggin to try to prove what she thought?
3. What made Ida more suitable than Oskar for the experiment?
4. What suggests that Dr Biggin really believed in the effects of the porridge?
5. What does Miss Bun think of the porridge? What is her opinion of her own cooking?
6. Why did Dr Biggin wink at the children when she asked Miss Bun to make risotto?

*Opinions*

*From what you read in the story who would think:*
1. *Paradurra megalocephala abyssiniensis* was the main food of giants
2. The Ogru were poor cooks
3. Miss Bun was a good cook
4. The Committee would be interested in the risotto?

# 37 The Young David Livingstone

1. It was barely light as a small sturdy boy trotted down the street towards the cotton factory; he was only ten years old, and he had to be at work by six o'clock, but this morning he was filled with excitement. It was the end of his first week at work, and in the evening he would proudly take home his first wages. He would hand it to his mother, but she had promised that he might keep back the price of a Latin grammar-book that he had seen in the window of a second-hand shop.

2. The boy was David Livingstone, second son of a poor family living near Glasgow. He bought his book and learned Latin as he stood at the spinning-machine. As he grew older, he worked at his lessons far into the night until he was able to go to college to study to be a doctor. His great desire was to go to China as a missionary and he knew that the work of spreading the Gospel would be greatly helped if he could also heal the sick. . . .

3. Alas for his hopes! War in China meant that it was impossible to send out missionaries for the time being. Greatly disappointed, he turned into a meeting hall one evening to listen to the famous missionary, Doctor Moffat, who was to speak about his work in South Africa. Sitting there, David heard Moffat say:

4. "On a clear morning, I can see from the hills near Kuruman, the smoke of a thousand villages where no missionary has ever been."
5. Livingstone's heart leapt when he heard these words, and at the end of the meeting, he stayed behind hoping to have a word with the doctor.
6. "Do you think, sir," he asked, "that there is work for me in Africa?"

(From *People in History* by R. J. Unstead)

### Questions

*Context clues*

*From clues in the passage, find the word which means:* (a) strong and well built *(paragraph 1),* (b) one sent to preach religion in a foreign country *(paragraph 2),* (c) the teachings of Christ *(paragraph 2).*

*Fill in the missing words*
Read the passage carefully. Twelve words have been missed out in the summary below. Suggest a suitable word for each blank.

David Livingstone started work in a ... 1 at the early age of ... 2. Out of his first pay he bought a ... 3 Latin grammar book.

He learned Latin while he worked at his ... 4 and in later years he ... 5 far into the night. His main wish was to become a ... 6 but he studied to qualify as a ... 7.

It was at the time of his ... 8 at not being sent to ... 9 that he went to hear Dr Moffat. Moffat spoke of many ... 10 which had never been visited by any ... 11. Livingstone asked if he might have the ... 12 to work in Africa.

*Inferences*

1. In paragraph 2 it is said that Livingstone came from a poor family. *What do you find in paragraph 1 to suggest his family was poor?*
2. *Read paragraph 1 again.* What suggests that David Livingstone was fit and strong when he was young?

*The reason why*

Complete each of the following sentences. Write out the whole sentence.
1. Livingstone worked far into the night because . . . .
2. David Livingstone could not go to China because . . . .
3. While listening to Dr Moffat, Livingstone became very excited because . . . .

*Figure of speech*

Livingstone's heart leapt. *(paragraph 5)*
Did his heart really leap? What does this expression mean?
When might your heart leap?

*Predicting outcomes*

1. What do you think Moffat would say to David Livingstone?
2. What do you think would have happened?
3. Would Livingstone be a more successful missionary because he was a doctor? Why?